And with the Gift Came Laughter

AND WITH THE GIFT CAME LAUGHTER

♥♥ ♥♥

ANN KIEMEL ANDERSON

Tyndale House Publishers, Inc.
WHEATON, ILLINOIS

First printing, July 1987

Library of Congress
Catalog Number 87-50543
ISBN 0-8423-0029-5
Copyright 1987 by
Ann Kiemel Anderson
Printed in the
United States of America

with special gratitude to:

virginia muir
my devoted, ingenious editor.

don and lorraine crewtzen
and dick and tomoe osborn
who so graciously have opened
their homes for me to hide away and
do my writing.

tim botts
the man whose creative edge has
especially endeared this book to me.

pat mings
my faithful, capable secretary,
who typed the first, rough draft.

my dearly loved parents
and mother-in-law
who gave tea parties and hours of
loving to taylor and brock while i wrote.

my dear sister, jan
who sits beside me with each book
and critiques the pages. without
her encouragement i would never
have completed a manuscript.

her husband, tom, and three sons
who share her with me
for days at a time.

will and my little sons
whom I love so profoundly.
without them, there would never
have been the story.

our compassionate, mighty God
who took my hand and led me
safely through the desert to the
laughter on the other side.

FOREWORD

This is a love story. It is a story of God's never-ceasing provision of healing for His children's bottomless well of needs and their cries for help. It is also a story of how one human being can extend a piece of herself to another human being, transcending her own pain and woundedness, to bring love into that person's life.

I am coming to realize more and more that children are brought into our lives to purify the essence of our love. The babies in this story have done more than any university education or any library of love stories could ever have done to teach these women what depth of surrender is involved in truly loving. Through great anguish, God led Ann past the road to motherhood most of us travel, and brought her to unwed, pregnant women who needed to be loved. She reached beyond her own emptiness and yearning and comforted them. And they in turn surrendered their own flesh—a significant sacrifice—to Ann and Will, people they felt could love their babies more completely, and began a new journey toward finding true self-love.

These are all brave women. They have made real love stories come to life in a world where, all too often, women choose easy answers and immediate solutions. We all want our lives to be love stories . . . and love is born out of a surrendered life.

Ann has two beautiful children brought into this world by other women. I have three children delivered out of my own womb. Through different avenues we have been given children to love. We are their care-takers—and, in a sense, they are ours.

JAN REAM
February 1987

INTRODUCTION

i have returned home—honolulu, hawaii—to write
about my experiences as a mother.

all my feelings about babies started right here, when
i was a little girl, and my father pastored a nazarene
church. dolls had always been our thing, jan's and
mine.

we played "pretend" for hours. putting pillows under
our blouses. experiencing pregnancy. babies crying.
we covered them at night, believing they actually
were cold. husbands called from work. we prepared
"dinners." hours and hours of play that seemed real.

my father would often go to the hospital to visit sick
people. jan's and my most vivid memory is sneaking
in beside him (in those days, children were not
allowed to visit), and finding the nursery. we stood
before the large glass window, mesmerized by the tiny
newborns, lined up side by side.

even when we were in high school, a couple who
worked with the teens at church had their fifth baby.
we idolized the mother. the baby. held them in the
highest esteem. the woman had produced the most
spectacular of all miracles: a baby!

jan, my twin, has come with me to honolulu, leaving
her three little sons and her husband. i have come
with brock, my younger one, and have left taylor with
his daddy and grandma jo. my parents are here—now

and
with
the
gift
came
laugh
·ter·

♥

retired, but still serving, at seventy, on a church staff. brock is for them to enjoy. jan, as always, comes to critique and inspire me page by page. i come to tell you my personal story.

there is a private place in my heart that is very tender, very sensitive to some of you who will read this book. some of you, as yet, have no children. you may be today where i have been—wrenched and grieved and aching for a child. please know that though God has blessed me with two little sons whom will and i love and cherish beyond description, i have not forgotten where you are. i have been through too much pain to forget your place. it once was my place.

stay with me through the story. remember, i believe for you!

i wonder what you would think if you had seen me two days before i got on the plane. at home with those two little sons. taylor (two and a half) and brock (one and a half) had been invited to a little friend's house to watch a special video cartoon. it takes much effort for me to make it out the door by 10 a.m. toys picked up. kitchen clean from breakfast. grocery list made. blankets folded and cribs straightened. my hair shampooed. babies in their car seats. clothes in the front seat to go to the dry cleaners.

we got to joshua's and the mothers ended up watching the cartoon while all the children played with toys in the back bedroom and begged for banana bread in the kitchen.

afterwards, brock went home with one of the young mothers, since he would be traveling with me for seven days. i took taylor, as a treat, to accompany me

and
with
the
gift
came
laugh
·ter·

♥

on errands. at the office he sat on my lap, playing
with the phone, while i shakily jotted notes. we met
two ladies for lunch and had barely been seated when
i realized taylor had diarrhea. time out. not for the
first time, i wondered who designs restaurant bath-
rooms. definitely not an experienced mother with a
sympathetic heart!

at the beauty shop, while craig cut my hair, taylor
took all the curlers he could find and lined them up
by size and color. all around the room.

we picked brock up and headed for the ice cream
shop. it was nap time, but i so love having fun. next
time i will know better. i ordered peppermint ice
cream, on sugar cones, for the babies. taylor began to
cry and protest, "i want white ice cream!"

"taylor, this has little candies in it. you will love it."

"no. no! i want WHITE ice cream."

finally i asked for a paper cup large enough to dump
all three cones into, and with both babies screaming
(brock,because he hadn't finished and taylor because
the ice cream was not white), i put them back into the
car seats, praying for calmness and patience and
wisdom. hating scenes. taylor finally got spanked.
(i *hate* spankings, but i believe in them for certain
occasions, and i seem to find these occasions more
often than i like, with a two-year-old.) home at last.
both boys quickly went down for naps.

later in the afternoon, while brock was still sleeping,
taylor and i were playing in my bedroom. when he
asked if he could make a mountain and play sailboats,
i nodded okay. so wanting him to have fun. not
wanting to squelch his creativity. within five minutes,
every chair he could find, including the high chair,

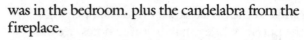

and
with
the
gift
came
laugh
·ter·

♥

was in the bedroom. plus the candelabra from the fireplace.

the phone rang. while i was talking briefly to a friend, the doorbell rang. taylor ran and opened the door to a woman i had never seen before. i stood, half-dressed and aghast, peeking around the bedroom door. before i could say good-bye to the lady on the phone, taylor said something about making our guest a playhouse, and he proceeded to pull all the pillows off the two sofas, covering most of the living room floor. by this time, brock had awakened, pulled off his diaper, darted out the front door, and was standing on the front porch.

it turned out that the woman had been sent by my husband to be interviewed for a secretarial job. he had been trying to call me to let me know she was coming, but i was on the phone. considering the absolute chaos that had developed within a ten-minute time span, i wondered if she would even consider the job—no matter what my evaluation might be.

so, i humbly write this book. my two-year-old is not completely potty-trained. his brother, eleven months younger, is moving into the "NO" stage. however, this is a love story. my childhood dream becoming reality. a story of laughter and celebration, of joy after sorrow . . . beauty for ashes . . . occasional exasperation . . . and utter inadequacy.

come with me. . . .

all my life, only one thing really mattered to me.

one thing, that is, next to knowing God. my minister father and my lovely, sophisticated mother taught me to embrace Him above all else.

all my life, i just wanted to be a mother. every year i received only one Christmas gift that truly counted: a doll. not a barbie or a fashion doll, but a baby doll. my mother spent hours searching every toy department in town to find the most-like-a-baby doll available. each year she seemed to come up with a better one. one that drank its bottle. one that wet. that was limp and could nestle into your neck. one that sucked its thumb.

jan and i agree that our most

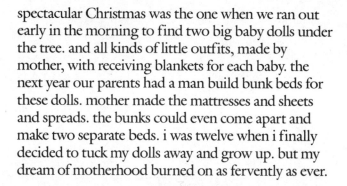

and
with
the
gift
came
laugh
·ter·

♥

spectacular Christmas was the one when we ran out early in the morning to find two big baby dolls under the tree. and all kinds of little outfits, made by mother, with receiving blankets for each baby. the next year our parents had a man build bunk beds for these dolls. mother made the mattresses and sheets and spreads. the bunks could even come apart and make two separate beds. i was twelve when i finally decided to tuck my dolls away and grow up. but my dream of motherhood burned on as fervently as ever.

at thirty-five i married. i had waited, determined not to make a mistake, and though i had dated some very sharp, attractive men, it was only when will anderson appeared that i knew the right man had come.

will was born in houston, texas, when his father was in law school. later the family moved to idaho, where will and his dad developed what was at that time the largest seed potato ranch in the world. twelve years ago, bill anderson died.

will moved to the ranch as soon as he finished graduate school, but after our wedding in boston, we bought a new home in idaho falls, fifty miles from the ranch. will's mother, jo, whom i love, lives seven miles away at the "home place."

will and i decided we wanted to try for a baby right away. he was thirty-eight and had waited all those years for me. traveling the world and being absorbed by business, he had never before been ready to settle down. to have children. now we shared a common dream.

i had had lots of experience learning that dreams are challenging. that their fulfillment is hard. several years before, i had dreamed of becoming a marathon

and
with
the
gift
came
laugh
·ter·

runner, and at thirty-four years of age had donned
sneakers and old shorts and started out the door one
morning to become a runner. six and a half months
later, with blood-and-guts determination, i ran my
first 26.2-mile course in israel. seven weeks after that,
in new orleans, i qualified for the boston marathon—
and eventually i ran eight marathons all over the
world. it was the hardest thing i had ever done, but
with enough heart . . . and God's love . . . and relent-
less training, i accomplished it. and it had been
somewhat like that when i was working my way
through college. always, the challenge of a dream.

somehow, though, i had assumed that the dream of
having a baby would be easier to attain. that the
hardest part had been waiting so many years for the
right man to be my husband. but i quickly learned the
word "infertility." strictly speaking, of course, i was
not infertile. i could become pregnant all right, but
each time, i would miscarry during the first few
weeks. during one year i was hospitalized eight times
with pregnancy-related problems. i grew to fear
anesthesia far more than any 26.2-mile course, and i
developed a feeling of defectiveness that consumed
me until i had very little self-esteem left.

what a mistake it had been to base all my security
upon performance and success! in this situation, no
matter what medication, what shots, what torment i
subjected my body to through surgeries and other
procedures, i could not make a baby. i was completely
stripped and broken. and i was suddenly empty
enough of myself to see God in a way i had never seen
Him before.

after miscarrying baby after baby . . . after will's
determination not to adopt the first newborn offered
us (which nearly finished me) . . . after will's agreeing

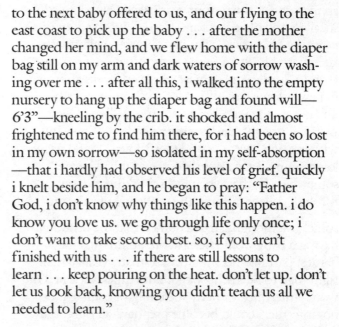

and
with
the
gift
came
laugh
·ter·

♥

to the next baby offered to us, and our flying to the
east coast to pick up the baby . . . after the mother
changed her mind, and we flew home with the diaper
bag still on my arm and dark waters of sorrow wash-
ing over me . . . after all this, i walked into the empty
nursery to hang up the diaper bag and found will—
6'3"—kneeling by the crib. it shocked and almost
frightened me to find him there, for i had been so lost
in my own sorrow—so isolated in my self-absorption
—that i hardly had observed his level of grief. quickly
i knelt beside him, and he began to pray: "Father
God, i don't know why things like this happen. i do
know you love us. we go through life only once; i
don't want to take second best. so, if you aren't
finished with us . . . if there are still lessons to
learn . . . keep pouring on the heat. don't let up. don't
let us look back, knowing you didn't teach us all we
needed to learn."

hearing his prayer, i shuddered. at first i felt anger.
how could he pray that way? how dare he tell God to
give us more sorrow if He needed to? it was MY
body that was getting all the needles. MY body losing
the babies. MY little-girl, lifelong dream being
shattered.

but very quickly, in the utter silence of that little
nursery, i knew in my heart that will's prayer was
truth. i said "yes" to it as i clung to his big, strong
hand. i walked out of that room a freed woman—
made new. i began really to love and enjoy will.
idaho. new friends.

and the first miracle happened.

a young single woman on the east coast was pregnant.
she was a college graduate. had a responsible position.
the father of the baby persuaded her to go to an
abortion clinic, but before the procedure could be

and
with
the
gift
came
laugh
·ter·

♥

done, she stumbled out of the clinic, sobbing. "i can't go through with this." at home, in her bedroom, she turned on the radio and heard me on a network interview. her heart was touched. for me. when we least expect God's surprises, they come . . . this one in the form of a telephone call.

"ann, this is liz." (of course, that's not her real name.) "i'm twenty-seven. i'm six months pregnant. i have reviewed all the options, and i know i must give my baby up. i know it's not right for me to marry the father, and it's so important to me that my baby have a father. would you and will be interested?"

six weeks before her due date, liz drove across the country, with her father, to idaho falls. she loved her dad, and he didn't want her to make the trip alone. he flew back home and we found her a place to stay, with a close friend of ours not far from our home.

every afternoon, liz worked in my office, organizing the library, typing a little, helping in many ways. she didn't want to sit around with nothing to do. it was terrific for my secretary and me. liz got a feel for my world. for the people who read my books. for my heart. we often had lunch together. laughed together. we anticipated every doctor's appointment, and what the report would be. she loved will, and he, in his no-nonsense, down-to-earth way, loved her and felt totally at peace about the process. about the prospect of this baby's becoming ours.

liz asked me to be her lamaze coach during labor. although i had been pregnant, i had no real idea of what labor and delivery would be like. it was awesome . . . yet exciting . . . to think of sharing all this with liz.

we talked a lot. i continually asked her what she was

and
with
the
gift
came
laugh
·ter·

♥

feeling. any ambivalence? any doubts? we both loved ice cream, and often we would laugh and chat about our dreams over ice-cream cones. she seemed well aware of the loss. of the sacrifice of releasing the baby. she appeared happy. contented with her decision. steadfast.

will and i repeatedly told her, "please, don't feel pressured. you are not in a corner you can't get out of. we love you. if you change your mind, we will still love you. we have been through a lot of loss . . . but what is right for the baby is right for you . . . and for us."

we meant it. i do not believe she ever felt pressured. of course, after all we had lost, some creeping fear could have invaded my peace and surrender. but i just refused to let it in. after one survives a certain level of pain, one becomes tougher. more confident and strong. i knew i would survive, no matter what. i truly believed that God is good.

liz did beautiful little things. on mother's day, a week before she went to the hospital, she gave will and me a mother's day card, praising us as parents. telling us of her admiration for us and of her joy. it was one of those flawless sundays. breezy. warm sunshine. we took a picnic lunch to the snake river. my mother-in-law came . . . the baby's grandmother. we all laid hands on liz's stomach. we each prayed for her . . . for the baby. we believed the baby could hear us and could feel our love and unity. liz prayed for us, the parents. we cried together. hugged. in my heart i could hardly believe that i would soon hold a tiny newborn and call it mine.

one night a week, for six weeks, liz and i went to the lamaze classes. we told our story to no one but the

and
with
the
gift
came
laugh
·ter·

leader. everyone assumed that liz was an unwed mother who planned to keep her baby and that i was a friend helping her through it. liz always looked darling—she is very petite, with hair the color of mine, with some natural curl. she carried the baby right out in front. like a basketball. she loved a wholesome diet. exercise. she was disciplined. methodical. meticulous.

as i sat in the circle, with the lamaze teacher in front, i had so many emotions. i loved liz deeply. i felt so bonded, so close to her. i already loved this baby in her. loved "it" profoundly. yet, at moments i wished that baby were within me. that i could experience the labor and delivery. i was in awe of these women around me. the ultimate success in life, i thought, was to be pregnant and close to delivery.

"rub her arms. run your hands up and down her legs," the teacher instructed. i was embarrassed. i felt so shy. so funny. i had never rubbed another woman's arms and legs. but liz was so sweet, so relaxed. she seemed so happy and secure that i was with her that i would begin to forget my inhibitions and become absorbed with this task of helping bring "our" baby into the world.

after class liz would hug me and go home, carrying her pillow and blanket. and i would go home to will, smiling. telling him what a strange but wonderful experience this was. we would laugh together.

one evening in the class, a darling girl who had always sat next to us, with her husband, said, "are you ann kiemel?"

"yes, i am."

"i've read one of your books! someone sent it to me."

and
with
the
gift
came
laugh
·ter·

♥

her baby, a little girl, was born two days after liz's, and diane and i have been good friends ever since.

the closer it came to liz's due date, the more excited and scared i became. could i really be enough for her in labor? i had heard horror stories about women who screamed and became hysterical. i felt like such a novice at this.

i started thinking about a certain night i will never forget. it is as vivid as if it were yesterday. jan, my twin sister, was expecting her first baby. it was what we had always dreamed about, but had hardly believed it was possible. we had never felt good about our appearance, because we had grown up in hawaii among such beautiful olive-skinned people. would men even look our way, much less want to marry us? would we ever become mothers, with real live babies?

jan telephoned. she had just gone to the hospital. was in a labor room. feeling wonderful, really. her water had broken, but she felt that this was going to be much easier than she had thought. i was in boston, preparing to drive to gordon, on the north shore, where i was to speak. it was january 22, 1977. i was overwhelmed with excitement. could this really be happening?

"women all around me are screaming and acting so emotional, ann. you wouldn't believe it. anyway, i'll call you in a little while and let you know how i'm doing."

after that, i heard nothing more. hours went by. i had given her the number where i would be staying, but the phone did not ring. my friend hattie and i left, in a blizzard, to drive to the church where i was to speak. the room was packed, and i rose to address the audience with barely enough poise to remember what to

and
with
the
gift
came
laugh
·ter·

♥

say. ("what's happening to jan? is she having an awful
time like all those other women? screaming? it's been
hours and hours. why haven't i heard?")

when i finished my speech, they took an offering.
i left the platform quietly and asked for a telephone.
i had a knot in my stomach. i felt sick. ("i must reach
jan. i must find someone . . . tom . . . or a nurse . . .
to tell me what is happening. is she all right?")

"st. luke's hospital. . . ."

"please, could i have the labor and delivery room? . . .
this is ann kiemel. i am jan ream's sister. we are twins.
very close. it is so important to me to know how my
sister is. can you tell me?"

"she is in recovery. she is doing fine."

"in . . . recovery? she's had the baby?"

"yes, she has."

"well, what was it? you can tell me. she'd want me to
know!"

"it's a boy."

"a BOY? really? a real little boy?"

"yes. . . ."

"he's normal and everything?"

"i believe he's perfect," the nurse responded with a
little laugh.

a boy. a nephew. she did it! jan and God did it. i ran
back to the platform. they were just finishing the
offering. i grabbed the microphone, and with tears
streaming down my face, i announced the sweetest-
sounding news in the world.

and
with
the
gift
came
laugh
·ter·

♥

jan had prepared me for liz's delivery. "ann, after i called you that night from the labor room, i became sicker and sicker. it wasn't long before i was screaming, too, digging my fingers into tom's arms. be prepared for anything."

may 16, 1984. at 6 a.m. the phone rang. it was liz. her water had broken. the doctor had said to come in within an hour. this was the day. it had finally arrived. i will never forget the excitement of that moment. will went to his office, asking me to call him when it was time for him to come to the hospital for the actual delivery. liz wanted us both to be there when the baby was born.

she had chosen the birthing room. it was similar to a regular bedroom, with rocking chair . . . cradle . . . a homey atmosphere where they allowed everyone to be together during delivery. however, when liz and i got to the hospital, that room was in use, so we were put into a regular labor room until the other one could be readied for liz. she was garbed in hospital gown and hooked up to all the monitors, to catch the baby's heartbeat and other statistics . . . and we began our long ordeal.

it started slowly. she was soon moved to the birthing room, and the contractions became more and more obvious. will stopped in a couple of times, offered brief prayers, and chatted for awhile before returning to the office. i had brought a tape recorder with a praise tape, but eventually we forgot the recorder, and i just sang soothing songs in my simple voice. we had the breathing down almost perfectly.

liz's main nurse was named joyce. once when she stopped by the room she said to me, "how often do

and
with
the
gift
came
laugh
·ter·

you help women in labor? you are very good at it!"

i smiled gratefully. "oh, this is my first time. i was feeling very unsure of myself. thanks for the encouragement."

since that day, joyce—with five children of her own to look after—has become one of my favorite people and often has traveled as my babies' nurse when i have taken them with me on speaking trips.

for eighteen hours liz groaned and breathed and rested and gasped with pain, then started the breathing exercise again. i became so absorbed in helping this lovely, amazing young woman that i forgot time and space and the need for food. i even lost touch with the reality that this was, we hoped, my own baby she was delivering. i took all the breaths with her. i rubbed her legs. her arms. her back. i held her head. i fed her ice chips. she would whisper faintly, "sing . . ." and i'd sing. doctors and nurses came and went, and i sang around them.

she didn't want me to leave her for a moment. i shifted around the little wires and the other paraphernalia. once in awhile, i would catch the doctor's eye. (he is my own obstetrician-gynecologist and as professional and skilled as they come.) i was not sure, but i thought his eyes spoke of deep concern. i just kept concentrating on liz. i knew that if a problem developed, he would let me know soon enough. it had been liz's hope and ours that we could all be together at delivery . . . but suddenly the doctor walked in, took a look at the monitor, and said, "baby is in trouble. you are not dilating fast enough and the baby is getting very tired. we are going to take you in for a c-section immediately."

and
with
the
gift
came
laugh
·ter·

♥

instantly the scene changed. liz, pale and worn from many hours of labor, held my hand until they whisked her down the hall and behind closed doors. in tears, i ran to find will in the waiting room. every time, something had gone wrong—with the baby i was carrying or one we were to adopt. now i feared it was happening again.

it was about 11:35 p.m. literally within moments, a nurse scurried down the hall with a bundle cradled in her arms and announced in a strong british accent, "mr. and mrs. anderson, you're the parents of a fine baby boy!" and she rushed on down the hall toward the nursery, while we stood motionless. eyes glistening with tears of joy. a boy. a son! all the losses seemed so insignificant. all the pain swept away. i wasn't tired any more. pam, my faithful secretary, was there to rejoice with us.

liz was still in surgery, so we were not allowed to see her yet. we raced down the hall toward the nursery. we were told to scrub and put on the gowns, and then we could go into the nursery and see him. hold him. there were babies everywhere. i hurriedly scanned each little basket. where was taylor?

we had already chosen his name. taylor jenkins anderson.

"taylor" for dr. kenneth taylor, who paraphrased *The Living Bible* and is the chairman of the board of tyndale house publishers. he prayed for me before i met will. he prayed at our wedding. we wanted this baby, boy or girl, to be named after him. to have a portion of his spirit of love and gentle strength.

"jenkins" for glenn jenkins at the ranch. a hearty, loyal

and
with
the
gift
came
laugh
·ter·

old man with piercing bright eyes, who was like a
father to will. he looked after things at the ranch as if
the land were his own. his wife, a remarkable lady,
had died about four months after will and i married.
will and i had stood by her as she lay in a coma in the
intensive care unit, and prayed with her and held her
hand. glenn is not particularly religious. tough and
rugged, with a great heart. we wanted this baby to be
partly his.

the nurse motioned for us to come where she was
standing, at the other side of the room. oh, that
miraculous moment when will and i stood, side by
side, and saw our little son for the first time. i still
cannot tell it without tears in my eyes. moments old.
tetracycline in his eyes. light brown hair. solid and
sturdy and robust looking. eight pounds, nine ounces.
no wonder he had had a hard time getting here! i
knelt on the nursery floor and reached through the
hole in the side of that little basket. i gently stroked
his arm and hand.

"taylor . . . ," i whispered.

instantly he jerked his little head to the side, eyes wide
open, trying to see me through the tetracycline. i will
never forget that instant response to my voice. i
began to sing softly, "God loves you . . . and i love
you . . . and that's the way it should be."

will, misty-eyed, gazed down at our baby. "ann, i
never realized how homely newborn babies are, until
i see all these other babies compared to taylor. taylor
is beautiful!"

i couldn't help laughing. most people think their baby
is the most beautiful one, and will surely did.

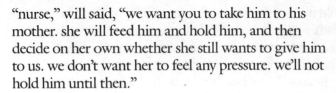

"nurse," will said, "we want you to take him to his
mother. she will feed him and hold him, and then
decide on her own whether she still wants to give him
to us. we don't want her to feel any pressure. we'll not
hold him until then."

the nurse looked amazed. she glanced at me. i nodded
"yes" . . . i agreed with will. i agreed . . . with a little
tremble in my heart.

the nurses had all been in awe of this whole experience. liz and i sharing the labor together. will a part
of it. no secrets. no snatching the baby away. love and
warmth and a spirit of peace, not anxiety.

before going home, we slipped back to the recovery
room and spent time with liz. she was radiant. calm.
she and i hugged each other and prayed. we told her
about our message to the nurse. it must have been
2:30 the next morning before we stopped off at an
all-night convenience store for hot dogs, then
stumbled home, called family, and fell into bed. i was
so weak with emotion and exhaustion that i felt as if i
had delivered the baby myself!

it was midmorning before we could get out of bed
and hurriedly start to dress. i was scared and excited.
liz had shown no sign of ambivalence. but that was
before the baby. i was not uptight. not on edge. i had
learned to say "yes" to God's plans. i just knew there is
always risk when one truly loves.

the attorney was coming to the hospital, as was the
judge—millie, a dear friend, who was doing this as a
special favor. (now, every girl must go to the courthouse and appear before the magistrate herself.) we
had worked out all the plans beforehand.

will and i went along first, into liz's room. her hair

and
with
the
gift
came
laugh
·ter·

was brushed, her face shining. she held taylor in her arms. i sat on the edge of the bed and will stood beside me.

"liz, what are you feeling?" i asked gently.

tears filled her eyes and spilled down her cheeks. i knew they were on my face too, but i didn't move. i loved that baby so much, yet it seemed i loved liz almost as much. she was so brave. had fought such a good fight. not once, through all those hours of hard labor, had she cried out or complained. not once did she lose control. she felt almost as much my child as taylor did.

"ann, isn't he beautiful? oh, ann, i carried him for you. . . ."

quietly, simply, she lifted the little bundle to me. i tucked him under one arm and threw my other arm around liz. they were both a part of me forever. i kissed and kissed taylor's little face and then handed him to will. big, strong, wonderful will. what a great father he would be. dashing and brave and no-nonsense, but kind and steady and humble enough to need God.

the attorney and the judge came in. with joy . . . with a feeling of victory in the midst of loss . . . liz signed. we could almost see love written on the walls and hear music in the air.

liz helped me dress him. blue cotton sacque with white lace and smocking. a bunting made by some ladies in canada—only one of dozens of lovely gifts sent by friends . . . readers of my books . . . people to whom i had spoken on my travels . . . all celebrating with us, as so many did later when brock came. an exquisite hand-knitted blanket will's mother had

and
with
the
gift
came
laugh
·ter·

♥

given. i left a packet of surprises by liz's bed. little things to find and enjoy and read in the next few hours while she lay there alone. a new nightie. the little gold heart, bought in israel long ago, that i'd always worn around my neck. a letter from my heart to hers.

will and i stood there, taylor in my arms. we looked at liz. how does one say "thank you"? how does one possibly grasp the magnitude of such a gift? with a mist in his eyes and passion in his voice, will said, "liz, we can never, ever, thank you enough. we love you."

i was a mother, receiving a gift. she was a mother, bestowing it. the power of that moment and the love it held for us all will live forever, to be recalled almost daily. never to be forgotten.

we went out into the bright, crisp spring day. cloudless sky. radiant sun. flags on poles. balloons flying through the air.

the little nursery had been waiting a long time for this one, chosen, beautiful, sacred gift.

♥ ♥
♥ ♥

the nursery
was ready.

drawers filled with clothes. plenty of bottles. a changing place on the kitchen counter.

i walked through the door of our home—thirty-eight years of age—with our one-and-a-half-day-old son. no one can prepare a woman for that moment. suddenly, instantly, life changes radically. even marriage does not bring the responsibility that a baby does—especially the first baby. it is all so new, and a baby is so tiny and helpless.

i wondered if i was capable of handling such an awesome responsibility. although i had played with dolls all through my childhood and had baby-sat my way through college, that could not compare with having a tiny life totally dependent on me twenty-four

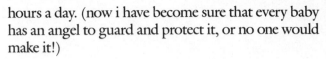

and
with
the
gift
came
laugh
·ter·

hours a day. (now i have become sure that every baby has an angel to guard and protect it, or no one would make it!)

our friends chuck and karen knocked on the door that first night and bounded in. karen, grandmother of several babies, picked taylor up and rewrapped him. she showed me a good way to rub his back and help him burp. she was so relaxed and so at ease that it made the difference for me on that crucial first day.

and how my days changed! no longer did i plop down and read a book whenever i felt like it. there were clothes to wash, bottles to prepare, clothes to fold . . . and then the next feeding. though i was sleepy at night, when taylor awakened every three or four hours, i experienced such sweet moments with him. the house was quiet. my little son nestled in my arms. my very own, real-live baby. i whispered to him and sang softly. right from the first we experienced such a bond and oneness.

because liz had had a c-section, she had to remain in the hospital for six days, then we brought her home to a different house. we felt she needed a fresh start, so we had moved all her things to the home of carol, a lovely lady who lived a few blocks from us. i would call and ask liz if she'd like me to bring taylor over, and she'd say, "oh, i'd love that!" i would dress him in baby blues and lace and white-smocked gowns, and hurry over. liz was still recovering from the surgery, but already she hardly looked as if she had just had a baby. we would ooh and ahh over him together. she would take pictures.

before she left idaho falls, she gave a beautiful brunch and invited the lamaze teacher and the nurses and some of our special friends. i dressed taylor up, and we sat together and shared our love and joy and

and
with
the
gift
came
laugh
·ter·

gratitude with them all. she and i took turns holding the baby. people were amazed that liz could be so selfless and that i could be so relaxed and feel so secure. some thought that i should fear her taking taylor back. it never crossed my mind.

will was determined that taylor be circumcised on the eighth day. that was biblical. one's blood clots better on that day than on any other day of our lives. i called around, and only one pediatrician was available to do circumcisions on that day. we carried taylor in. the nurse took him and the doctor cleared his throat.

"now, if the parents will step outside . . . this will take just a little time."

"we are staying with him," will stated. i nodded in agreement.

"oh, well . . . certainly . . . if that's what you'd like."

they strapped him down. taylor screamed in fear, and then in pain (at least, it surely looked as if it would hurt). and all the time i held his little hands and whispered to him and sang softly, over and over. will stroked his head and spoke in a reassuring voice. not for anything would we have missed being there with him!

after the first few weeks, i would roll out of bed each morning, worn out, and ask will, "how are you, honey?"

"i'm exhausted just listening to you getting up every night."

well, i figured if he was going to be tired anyway, i'd make it a little more worthwhile. "honey, i think we should take turns with these night feedings. you get up and take care of taylor once each night."

and
with
the
gift
came
laugh
·ter·

♥

he wasn't very enthusiastic, but it was hard to say "no." the next night, when taylor woke up at 3 a.m., i nudged will in the back.

"honey, this is your turn."

he sort of moaned and rolled out of bed. i lay there and got a little worried. he was so big. and taylor was so tiny. will didn't have much experience with newborns. it was very quiet out there, wherever he had taken the baby, so i decided to step out and just take a peek from the bedroom door to see what was happening.

3 a.m. cold tile kitchen counter. taylor lying on the bare counter. will held the bottle propped up with one hand while reading a book he held in his other hand . . . completely absorbed in his reading.

i burst into the room. "i can't believe it! pick that baby up! he'll grow up insecure if you feed him that way!" i really had to laugh. and i decided to go back to handling the night feedings myself. will fed him in the evenings. was always ready to change a diaper, wet or dirty.

we were a family. a real, live family. every night, we'd slip into the nursery together, say a prayer, watch taylor sleep, and then go to bed with the incomparable joy that down the hall, in a little white crib, slept our son.

my first speaking trip came when taylor was two weeks old. liz was just getting ready to leave town, and i did not know when we would see her again. i called her.

"liz, i fly to a couple of speaking appearances this morning, and i was wondering if you'd like to come and help me get him dressed for his first trip."

she came. i had all his little things laid out on the kitchen counter. he was bathed, rubbed with lotion, and then i handed him to her to dress. as she was getting the diaper under him, i looked in just in time to see an arching stream of urine fly through the air . . . through the open serving window between the kitchen and the living room . . . and onto the white living room carpet. we laughed hysterically as i tried to wash out the carpet and still get into the car and away without missing my flight.

i had embraced liz, in tears, and handed taylor to her for one last hug. she stood at the door of my house as we drove out of the driveway toward the airport. we waved to each other until the house was out of sight. she had let him become my little son, and i had to be brave enough to receive the gift without feeling so unworthy and overwhelmed that i couldn't enjoy it. she occupied such an intimate place in my heart, and it was hard for me to let her go. i loved her not only for taylor. i loved her for herself.

before we parted, i told liz that if, in the first fourteen or fifteen months of taylor's life, i was speaking anywhere close to where she was, i would call her. if she wanted to see him, i would love to have her. we had all decided that after that age, it would be better for taylor to wait until he's eighteen to know who she is and meet her. we very much want that to happen, for she is his roots, his beginning, and he will become even more whole as he has a chance to know his roots. if he, and she, both choose.

i was scheduled to speak at the same program with dale evans and debby boone (who had recently delivered twins) in chattanooga. in atlanta, i found myself seated next to dale on our flight. we had been great friends for a long time. what a shock she had

and
with
the
gift
came
laugh
·ter·

♥

when i walked onto the plane with my tiny new baby!
she knew all about adoption. when will was much
younger, he had read about this family and had
always wanted to do what dale and roy had done—
adopt many children and have a big, happy family.

"dale, the flight attendants will comment on what a
slim figure i have for having so recently given birth to
this tiny baby. please don't say anything. i'm so tired
of explaining on all the other flights. let's just have
fun, and let me enjoy the compliment!"

one by one the attendants admired the baby and
raved about my figure. i just smiled and said, "thank
you, thank you."

months later i was in california. i would be speaking
at a program for pat boone, and it was going to be
close to where liz lived. taylor was five months old,
and my best little friend and traveling companion. i
called liz, and she said she'd be in the audience and
would see me after the meeting.

hundreds of women. i shared my simple, earnest
story . . . of dreams and courage and ashes and tears.
of the miracle. the sunrise. i had my baby-sitter, who
was traveling with me, bring taylor to the platform.
he grabbed for me, and i wrapped him in my arms.
i felt inspired . . . compelled . . . to announce that his
birth mother was in the audience. i had no intention
of exposing her, yet i felt it was God's moment.

"liz, could you come up here? i want these ladies to
meet you."

she flew out of her seat. ran to the platform. weeping,
we threw our arms around each other. taylor clung to
me. i was his mommy. but love covered that room, as
women clapped and cheered and wept and celebrated
with us.

and
with
the
gift
came
laugh
·ter·

♥

all three encounters before his sixteenth month were
brief and light and fun. liz always brought me choco-
lates, because she knew i loved them, and something
special for taylor—a little book or toy. the good-byes
were not wrenching, but tender and warm and
relaxed, and often we laughed together over some
small, silly thing taylor did in the last few moments.

the last time we saw liz, it was in santa barbara. it was
harder, because we all knew that was it. taylor hung
on to me as liz broke down and wrapped her arms
around us both. seeing her tears, taylor suddenly
leaned over and kissed her on the cheek. a tender,
spontaneous gesture. as if to say, "i love you . . . i'm
not sure who you are, but we all belong. don't cry."
i had tears too as i boarded the plane and watched out
the window. my love for this young woman was so
strong, so deep. it is always hard to love but to let go.
to move on.

only with much loss . . . only when the gift has been
withheld or taken away so often . . . does the miracle
really stretch all boundaries of gratitude and overwhelming joy. only when the fulfillment of a dream
comes hard does one truly grasp, even in a small way,
the greatness of the real gift. the prize.

every friday
i go to the office.

one day, working through my mail,
i began to read a letter from a
young woman. it was neatly written.
articulate. she was twenty-three
years old. college degree. employed
in a glamorous profession. pregnant.

"ann, i am going to release my baby
for adoption, because it is so
important to me that there be a real
family for it to grow up in. i cannot marry the father. i am really just
not ready for marriage. i know
you have one child . . . but would
you and will be interested?"

karen (not her real name, of course)
had been brought up in a Christian
family but had chosen to go her
own way. a neighbor had loaned
her one of my books, and she loved
it.

although taylor was only seven

and
with
the
gift
came
laugh
·ter·

♥

months old, we already longed to have another baby, someone he could share life with, and karen's letter somehow felt right. it seemed positive to us that both babies would come from similar backgrounds.

i responded to karen's letter positively, but i shared with her the process we had used in our adoption of taylor. that will and i felt strongly about being there for the baby's birth and bonding as quickly as possible. would she be willing to come to idaho falls?

"oh, ann, could you be my coach through labor?" she wrote. "i would love for you and will to be in the delivery room, too."

it really did seem to be God's will . . . as we prayed each day, we felt such peace. karen told us that her father had died, but her mother supported her in the decision, feeling it was best for the baby, though of course it would be hard for her to release her first grandchild. later i met her mother in an airport. i had taylor with me . . . we all seemed to love each other.

we found another wonderful home for karen to stay in. private room and bath. a family. a dog. about four or five miles from our house. according to her due date, taylor would be eleven months old when this baby came. we were ecstatic. they would be close—almost like twins.

then came another surprise. about two weeks before karen was to come, i discovered i was pregnant. pregnant! would this make a difference in our decision about karen's baby? the more we prayed, the more we felt right about going ahead with the plans we had made. we had always wanted a big family. had married late. we could handle it . . . we'd get a nanny. provided, of course, that karen still wanted us to have her baby.

and
with
the
gift
came
laugh
·ter·

when one has experienced as much loss as we had, each gift becomes too valuable to refuse or give away.

but the surprises weren't over. at the doctor's office a few days later, he did an ultrasound and discovered i was carrying not one, but two babies. twins! we were in shock. God was giving us back some of what we had lost. we would have four babies . . . three different ages! well, we would get the help we needed . . . have a live-in nanny . . . our heads were whirling!

"karen, i must tell you some amazing news. i am pregnant with twins."

"ann!!!"

"karen, we still feel that it's right for us to have your baby, if you want us to. it seemed so right before this news. maybe God is going to give us our whole family at once. how do you feel about it?"

"i feel so excited, ann," karen responded. "my baby will grow up with lots of love and others to play with . . . and i still very much want you and will to be the parents."

we would never love our own flesh and blood more than we loved taylor. in fact, at moments, i feared we wouldn't be able to love these twins as much. he had brought the sunrise and starlight to our lives. we were so absorbed in our love for him—and we never even thought about his not coming from our own bodies. we were just delighted he was going to have siblings. we could be a real family. we didn't doubt for a moment that we would love karen's baby too.

i was feeling better than i had ever felt in a pregnancy. only somewhat tired. my waistline changed instantly, it seemed. i was so happy and fulfilled. taylor had become my best little friend. i would sometimes take him—even

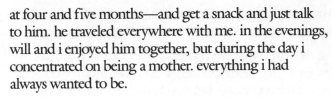

at four and five months—and get a snack and just talk to him. he traveled everywhere with me. in the evenings, will and i enjoyed him together, but during the day i concentrated on being a mother. everything i had always wanted to be.

beginning when taylor was just three days old, i would lay him on my lap and read the Bible to him . . . the psalms, day after day. i wanted him to love to read. we had named him for dr. taylor, who so dearly loves the Bible. we wanted that for taylor, too.

jan and i were in the process of writing our book, *struggling for wholeness*. i would get that book behind me and then completely focus my attention on taylor . . . and karen . . . and the babies that were to come.

karen arrived. another beautiful birth mother! taller than liz. her hair dark like mine too, with natural curl. fine features. fresh, cameo complexion. poised. articulate. liz had been disciplined about her eating habits . . . into health foods (how i admired that!). but karen was more like me . . . baked wonderful cakes. loved sugar! like me, neither liz nor karen had any weight problem, so we could all indulge ourselves a little. like liz, karen worked in my office. developed her own friends. was liked by everyone, just as liz had been. we loved getting some lunch together . . . or having her come over for dinner. sometimes she baby-sat taylor when we had to go out. we loved her!

"karen, after you leave here, i want you to meet liz. your babies are going to grow up together. it would be special if you could be friends too. i know you would like each other."

as i had with liz, i spent hours talking with karen about babies. especially hers to come, and taylor. would he

and
with
the
gift
came
laugh
·ter·

have a brother or a sister? hair? coloring? we loved to
dream together, and she knew how absolutely delighted
we were with the hope of her baby's becoming ours.
she saw how passionately we loved taylor.

"ann, this pregnancy is no longer a disaster. it now has
meaning and purpose. this baby is for you." both birth
mothers loved will. his strength. his love for God. his
zest for life. he was always into a new project. entre-
preneurial. fresh ideas. tremendous energy and momen-
tum. an outdoorsman. athlete. straightforward. they
both seemed to feel he would make the very best kind
of father for their babies.

in even six weeks, a birth mother and adoptive couple
can become such close friends. the camaraderie of such
an adventure can bond them together for life. for us, it
was important not to live together. not to become
enmeshed. to have both space and closeness. one of the
things i most loved about these girls was their indepen-
dence. they were happy . . . well adjusted. they didn't
need pampering. we were running a race, side by side,
with a common goal. a finish line. our hands and hearts
were joined, and we were cheering each other down the
home stretch.

karen would have the same doctor liz had had. he was
taking care of me, too. one saturday, will had flown out
of state on business, to be gone a couple of days. a
snowstorm had left idaho falls buried under drifts. ice
and snow closed the streets, and residents had been
asked not to go out. that saturday morning i awakened
with some cramping. though i had had a history of
miscarriages, it had never occurred to me that i might
miscarry this time. it had happened too many times
before. this time i had twins. surely God would not take
them. because i was an identical twin, i had always
wanted twins.

and
with
the
gift
came
laugh
·ter·

in the bathroom, i discovered i was spotting. panic gripped me in a way no words can describe. again, will was out of town, just as he had been when i had had previous miscarriages. although we have many friends in our community, many people we love, there was really no one i could call just then. many people find it hard to handle grief with someone. who would know how to help me?

my own doctor was out of town. i was devastated. i love and trust him, and though his partner is perfectly capable, he was almost a stranger to me. finally i called him. he told me to stay off my feet. i had been checked two days before and everything had seemed fine.

taylor was so sweet. it was such a comfort to have him playing by the couch. crawling around. he was such a miracle. God had given him to us . . . God had to be good.

by evening i was in so much pain, i could hardly stand it. the darkness that was falling outside was reflected in my trembling spirit. i had traveled this road many times before. i called karen, and it helped to talk to her, but the roads were so bad i didn't want her to come over. finally the doctor felt i should come into the hospital. my dear neighbor linda bravely volunteered to take me and to look after taylor. her little daughter, natalie, was having a slumber party, and the backseat was filled with giggling little girls. i knew and loved the little girls, but i was in so much pain and despair that i couldn't relate to their fun at all.

"o God . . . please, God . . . please . . . don't let me lose these babies," i prayed desperately.

linda dropped me at the emergency room door. she wanted to come in and stay with me; she assured me that the little girls could wait downstairs. but i didn't

and
with
the
gift
came
laugh
·ter·

feel good about it. linda and i are very close, but at that moment it didn't seem to matter whether anyone was with me. will was gone. it was really our struggle . . . our war against defeat. no one else could fight the battle with us.

as i walked into the hospital, another close friend—a nurse—was waiting for me. someone had called her. it was late, but she had hurried over to be with me. taking the elevator to the third floor—the maternity floor— brought back only bad memories for me. i had been there before. i was reliving a nightmare.

the doctor examined me. there was bleeding, but my cervix was still closed, and he felt i had about a 60 percent chance of saving the pregnancy. he was very kind and gentle. he wanted me to stay in the hospital overnight.

it was the longest, saddest night of my life. they had given me a pain shot, but the cramps were so severe that the medication only made me groggy in my pain. the bleeding would not stop, and for hours—all alone— i struggled to keep some degree of sanity. i'm sure i did not sleep an hour all night.

"God, i am a hannah, like hannah in the Bible. i dedicate these babies to you. will and i will raise them to love and honor you. you can have them for your service. oh, Jesus, please give me my babies."

but deep in my heart i had learned to say "yes." to agree with will's prayer: "do what you have to do, God. we are yours!" though i cried and begged, and twisted the sheet with my hands, there was a place deep within me where i said, "Jesus, Thy will be done . . . yes."

the doctor came in the next morning and said he had scheduled me for an ultrasound, to see what he could

and
with
the
gift
came
laugh
·ter·

♥

find. they began forcing me to drink many glasses of water that made me more violently sick than i already was. i already knew what he would find, anyway. i could tell. my breasts had lost their tenderness. my body felt different. any woman who has been there knows.

as i lay in the bed, with the radiologist rubbing the little instrument back and forth across my abdomen, i closely watched his face and the doctor's. the screen was just a blur to me, but their sad eyes and solemn faces told it all. my babies were gone. the excitement and thrill and beauty of life growing within me were gone, leaving twisted, knotted pain. how could i face another loss? how could i bear for will to come home and feel the disappointment too?

someone wheeled me back to my room, and there was karen, eight months pregnant, and a couple of other women. karen put her arms around me and we sobbed together.

"oh, ann, i'm so sorry. i wish it could have been my loss and not yours. i'm so sorry! ann, this baby in me is yours. i'm so happy it belongs to you. . . ."

God had known all along that my babies were going home to be with Him. this was all part of His plan. that was why we felt so strongly that karen's baby was to be ours, too. i clung to her and felt her swollen stomach pressing against mine—now so empty. what a combination of grief and gratitude. we were awesomely aware that God's wisdom and love were wrapped around all these babies in a way far beyond our understanding.

taylor was waiting for me when i got home. though i did not feel very well, i wanted to be alone with him. will would be home the next day, and i would have to prepare myself to tell him about what seemed to me to be my horrible failure. knowing he had to share the loss

and
with
the
gift
came
laugh
·ter·

too. one moment i would scream, "why?" the next, i would be snuggling taylor in my lap and realizing that "why?" was unnecessary. God had to be love to have given him to us. taylor was living proof to me of God's love and blessing, even in my wrenching grief.

will is strongest in the hardest moments. he wrapped his arms around me, and held me, and was calm and unshaken in his trust and faith. he watched taylor with an even more tender look in his dark eyes. he carried him around with an even more sacred sense of trust.

it took several weeks before i could stop crying in moments of quick reflection. death and loss are so hard. one moment there is life and promise and blessing. the next moment—darkness and a feeling of curse. one day, maternity clothes . . . joyfully proud. the next day, you can't bear to see them . . . would rather not bother to get dressed at all, but just hide.

a week later i decided to go to the office. as i was walking up the steps, a lovely woman i know was coming down. she obviously had heard about my most recent loss. she was stunned to see me and was speechless. stammering a brisk "hello," she turned quickly and nearly ran the other way. it left me with a terribly hollow feeling. rather than addressing my loss, she ignored it, and me. it would have meant so much if she had just talked about it and had let me tell her my feelings.

♥♥
♥♥

now, more than ever, we began to anticipate karen's delivery.

it was so healing to know we would soon hold another baby in our arms. she seemed as excited as we were. i had bought taylor a new bed, a crib, with drawers, that could be made into a junior bed later. the new baby would have the white crib. and many new things. i wanted the second baby to have everything special, too, so i bought new sheets and bumpers, and fresh receiving blankets. we waited to see if it was a boy—who could wear taylor's lovely, still-almost-new things—or a girl, for whom i would have to go shopping!

taylor was only eleven months old, but he was already walking. he had tremendous motor skills. and was so bright. it was as if God knew just how to prepare him for

and
with
the
gift
came
laugh
·ter·

♥

another baby. he immediately loved his new bed. the first three months, i would keep the new baby in a bassinet just outside our bedroom door, as i had done with taylor. we hoped that later they would both sleep in the nursery. we would have to see how it worked.

every night i fell into bed, exhausted . . . but in laughter. i would remind will to enjoy one more good night's sleep, because he might not have any for a long time after the baby was born. as i had prayed for liz, i now prayed for karen that she would go into labor in the morning, when we were both rested and fresh. God answered my prayers both times.

"ann," karen called excitedly about seven o'clock on the morning of april 19, 1985. "i'm having contractions, and the doctor wants us to come in as soon as we can get ready."

the morning we had been waiting for! will and i were ecstatic. he went on to work, at least for a while. my wonderful neighbor took taylor, still in his pajamas and wrapped in a warm blanket. i picked karen up and we laughed and exulted all the way to the hospital. she was a little scared, as liz had been. not knowing what to expect. not looking forward to pain. i was more at ease and more experienced in my assigned role. karen had decided with the doctor that she would have an epidural. that would not be done until she had dilated six centimeters.

the nurse hooked her up to the monitor. several nurses were there who had been there last time, and they were elated to watch us go through this kind of experience again. they were even more in awe that a second beautiful young woman seemed to love us and want to give us her baby.

and
with
the
gift
came
laugh
·ter·

karen was having contractions, but the nurse
suggested we go for a good brisk walk . . . eat a little
breakfast . . . and then come back. we walked and
talked, stopping at the pancake house. karen ate eggs
and bacon and two pancakes . . . we hoped afterward
that it wasn't a mistake! i should have eaten more than
i did, for i would be very hungry before this day was
done.

when we got back to the hospital, karen was hooked
up again and put in one of the familiar little labor
rooms. the doctor had okayed will's being in the
delivery room, and with an epidural, we could not be
in the birthing room. the english nurse with the
strong accent, who had announced taylor's birth, was
the key nurse for karen. she was a lovely lady, but a bit
brisk and abrupt. at times, i had to be assertive to
keep her from pushing me out of the room.

karen's labor went much more quickly and smoothly
than liz's. within about three hours, she was ready for
the epidural. an anesthetist came in and injected the
fluid into the spine, numbing her from the waist
down. it would make the labor more painless, but it
never did totally take effect with karen. she, too, was
extremely brave and stoic. never panicked. never cried
out. we clung together, running up that steep hill to
the victory line of delivery. there in the labor room . . .
just the two of us . . . in the middle of labor, karen
totally surrendered not just her heart, but her whole
life to Jesus.

"oh, ann, i so much want my life to count. i want it to
be different. i long for my baby to grow up close to
God, and i want to be close to Him too."

i was so full of love for karen . . . so completely
absorbed in helping her through this delivery . . .

and
with
the
gift
came
laugh
·ter·

♥

i sometimes lost touch with the fact that this baby would be ours. i cared not only about this moment for her, but her entire future. i longed for her, as i did for liz, to be whole. to be healed from this experience . . . strong, not crippled and bitter.

will stopped by, and we prayed together. one tends to lose track of time and place and food in the labor room, but shortly before five o'clock in the morning, the doctor announced that karen was ready for the delivery room. i could just see the baby's head, and even in the stress of the moment, karen and i were excited that the baby had hair!

will and i quickly donned our hospital garb . . . caps, gowns, shoes. we had had the gall to call bill, a dear friend, and ask if he could possibly come with a camera. if they refused to let him into the delivery room, he could snap pictures of the baby from the doorway and on the way to the nursery. when taylor was born, a television station had brought a camera and had taken video shots of his birth for a tv special i was doing. karen thought it was a wonderful idea for bill to come.

while i was helping karen push, every now and then i would look up and see that will was no longer standing behind the doctor. i smiled to myself. my husband—hot-dog skier, mountain climber, former race car driver—was probably a little faint and quietly going out for some air. not wanting anyone to notice. later he confessed, with a grin, that he did have a couple of moments of feeling lightheaded. but he was right there when the baby's head popped out. all along, the doctor had predicted a seven-pound baby, but when i saw the head, i knew this baby was bigger than that.

and
with
the
gift
came
laugh
·ter·

in another instant that husky little baby was out, and i screamed first, "it's a boy!" nine pounds, one ounce . . . lots of black hair . . . strong, sturdy physique that looked a lot like taylor's at birth. karen had requested that the doctor first hand the baby to me, but my arms were around karen and we were in tears.

"oh, ann, you have a son. another son. i'm so happy."

"karen, thank you, thank you, thank you! he's beautiful."

i went to hold my new baby son. wet from birth, but quiet and relaxed. i held him tightly and looked at will.

"honey, Jesus takes, and Jesus gives, and everything Jesus does is good."

our eyes were shining. the clock read 5 a.m. i handed the baby to will. at the doorway stood bill, father of one and with another on the way, snapping pictures. only later, when he picked up the film and the pictures were all black, did he realize there had been something wrong with the camera. we were disappointed, but still touched that bill had come at such an hour and that the memories were stored in our minds and hearts forever. no could take them away.

karen and will and i stayed in the delivery room for a long time. i laid the baby on her for a few moments for her to enjoy his beauty and specialness. God's creation . . . and hers. i cuddled him and, unaware of the doctors and nurses, sang to him what i had sung to taylor many times. . . .

oh, let the Son of God enfold you
  with His wonder and His love.
let Him fill your life and satisfy your soul.

and
with
the
gift
came
laugh
·ter·

♥

oh, let Him have the things that hold you,
  and His Spirit like a dove,
will descend upon your life and make you whole.

wholeness. that is what we most desire for our two
little sons. that will come not only in a faith in God,
and in our attempt at good, consistent parenting, but
in helping them to feel loved by their birth mothers
and in encouraging them, at eighteen years of age or
older, to meet them. we believe everyone should have
a sense of his or her beginnings.

will and i kissed karen, and, with the baby in will's
arms, we walked to the nursery. he was beautiful and
healthy and perfect. another little son. taylor would
have a brother. our hearts were overwhelmed with joy
and thanksgiving.

brock kiemel anderson. his name. "brock" for a close
friend of ours, bill brock. he and penny do not have
children, but they love ours as if they were their own.
every so often we spend weekends together, hiking
and shopping. will and bill working out at the fitness
center.

"kiemel" for my minister father. now an old man. but
holy, a prayer warrior. my mother, smart and full of
pizzazz, would laugh and say my father was so
heavenly minded, he was almost no earthly good. we
all loved him for that. she would remind us over and
over that we (herself included) would make it to
heaven because of daddy and his love and prayers.

karen had asked if i could come back a little after
noon and bring the baby into her private room for his
first feeding. i could hardly wait. will and i went back
to the nursery one more time after seeing karen in
recovery, and then went home to fall into bed about 8
a.m. i left taylor with my neighbor so we could sleep.

after each birth, i was completely spent, yet so excited i could hardly relax.

and with the gift came laugh ·ter·

i also knew we would tell karen what we had told liz—that she could still keep the baby. will and i both felt strongly about this, and though i never really feared the decision, there was still that tiny, quiet, nagging thought, "what if?"

back in karen's room, we passed brock back and forth. she loved his name. we spent hours talking about how beautiful and perfect he was. she was radiant. she had always been beautiful, but she looked more exquisite than ever after the birth. she was not afraid to cry. and i was not afraid to let her. tears are impor-tant . . . tears of joy. of awe that she had borne this amazing child . . . tears of wrenching grief and sadness. sadness that everything was not perfect in her life. that she felt deeply she must release him. that it was best for him. but loving him so—an actual piece of herself. i encouraged her to share all those feelings with me, and i tried never to talk her out of them to protect myself.

will's mother came to the hospital. so did neighbors and friends who had grown to love karen, even as many had grown to love liz. they brought her little gifts. for weeks karen had been working, in secret, knitting a beautiful white, lacy blanket. a gift from herself to her baby . . . from her to me. a gesture of immense love and care.

sunday morning brock was two days old. the attorney was to come, bringing the release papers for karen to sign so we could take brock home. she was going to bill and laurie's, a different home from the one where she had stayed before the birth. another new begin-ning. taylor was at the hospital with us, in our arms,

and
with
the
gift
came
laugh
·ter·

eleven months old. hair brushed in a curl. dressed in a beautiful new outfit from sally in boston.

will and i went in to talk to karen. to remind her that this was her choice. that we would love her, no matter what. she understood . . . and still signed. i asked her if she'd like to go into the nursery with me, and together we would dress brock to go home. karen on one side, i on the other, we put him into the same beautiful lace-trimmed, smocked gown that taylor had come home in. wrapped in the exquisite blanket she had made. april 21, 1985.

on the way home, will and i slipped into church, for babies were being dedicated that morning, and we wanted to offer him, immediately, to God. six weeks later, dr. ken taylor—for whom taylor was named— came to idaho falls. my parents came too, and we had a private dedication then for both boys. (my father had dedicated taylor when he was a month old, but we wanted all the dedications we could fit in!)

will's mother, jo, had prepared an elegant luncheon in her large living room, and we all met there after the morning service. karen, some close friends, the babies. taylor seemed—and was—still a baby himself. he bounced around in his little white baby shoes. his skin so fair. his eyes so blue. brock's hair was black. his skin very olive. today, both have natural curls. brock's hair has turned to a light brown. no one can tell they are not blood brothers. they will both be tall and well built, like their daddy. taylor's eyes blue like mine. brock's brown like will's.

on monday we were to go with karen to the magis-trate, at the courthouse, when she would sign the final papers, releasing parental rights. on this sunday afternoon i said again to karen, "will told me to tell you he stands with me in this. this little baby is still

and
with
the
gift
came
laugh
·ter·

yours. i can pack his prettiest things in a little bag and dress him up and let you take him on the airplane tomorrow. you are not trapped in a corner you can't get out of. we are committed to you, forever, no matter what you choose."

i spoke quietly, gently . . . meaning every word. this baby belonged to God. will and i never wanted to demand anything that was not meant to be ours. our hands were open. adoptive parents-to-be should never pressure a birth mother. it is an awesome, holy decision between her and God. our job is to give a birth mother all the room she needs to make the decision. usually (not always) she will come to the right conclusion, if given enough space.

karen threw her arms around me. "oh, ann, i know you really mean that. that is why i love you so much. you genuinely care about me. but if i kept brock, i'd never feel right about it. i would always know i had failed him. you are the perfect family for him. i haven't changed my mind. it is just so much harder than i thought it would be."

what a difficult moment . . . what a courageous woman. karen had kept asking herself the last twenty-four hours, would she ever be able to have another baby? if she did, would it be this beautiful . . . this good and sweet? such natural questions. so real and vulnerable . . . so poignant the struggle.

when will and i, with karen, taylor, and brock, entered the courtroom, we discovered the same judge who had done the final adoption process for taylor. he himself had a son named taylor, and he confided in us that "brock" was a name he had always wanted to use. our friend millie, the judge, slipped into a backseat. we were all dressed up. will carried taylor. i held

and
with
the
gift
came
laugh
·ter·

♥

brock. it was a holy, sacred moment. a gift. we had not fought and demanded. only trusted.

we were all sworn in, and then the judge asked karen, "have you been coerced?"

"no."

"are you on any kind of drug or medication that might alter your thinking?"

"no."

"are these the parents you want for this baby?"

"yes."

then he asked will and me questions. will's voice was strong and steady. my heart was beating fast, and i was amazed at the strength i heard in my own words. we loved this mother. we loved this baby. we loved our other baby. we wanted very much to be a family. a family of four. our attorney, tom, who knows just how to do his job, was there to represent us.

will says that when there is a decision to be made, the hard decision is often the right one. once karen had finally and irrevocably made her decision—though it was hard—she became a new person. the awesome reality of her choice was there before her—but she was filled with the freedom and joy and peace that come when one knows she has done the right thing. i've faced those moments of hard decision, too. when i walked away from a man i cared about because i knew he was not the right one for me . . . when i said "no" to a glamorous job because i felt God had something better in store for me. it's a time of loss and grief, but dignity and power begin to grow in one's character when one does the right thing.

often i am surprised when i hear people say, about an adopted child, "that poor girl. no wonder she has

and
with
the
gift
came
laugh
·ter·

such a hard time. her mother rejected her." or hear an adopted child say, "i will always wonder why my mother rejected me. it's ruined my whole life." people need to know . . . adopted children need to be taught . . . that for most birth mothers, giving up a baby is not an act of rejection. it is the most selfless, courageous, brave deed they can do. it is laying aside their own desires and longings, to bestow on that baby something greater and better than they can provide. for almost all birth mothers, a piece of themselves dies in that surrender. they understand that life is hard to deal with. that without both a father and mother . . . financial security . . . a stable, loving relationship . . . opportunities for education and culture . . . things that might otherwise never be within the child's reach . . . the child might not be able to become all God intended him to be. never yet have i met a birth mother who thoughtlessly gave her baby away.

we have a friend who adopted a baby girl. although will and i had nothing to do with that adoption, the parents shared with us a beautiful letter they received from their baby's birth mother. it reveals so clearly what is in most birth mothers' hearts regarding the babies they relinquish. here are a few lines from that letter:

"i prayed fervently that God would prepare a very special family for 'our girl,' and i was not reluctant to ask for much, with all the trimmings, on her behalf . . . i want her to feel the deepest sense of belonging and security and acceptance and unconditional love that you can give . . . of course, i truly wish that i could have been able to be the one to provide for her as she grows, but i cannot change the way things are—and i would not take her from you if i could, as things are now. but i will always love her with all my

and
with
the
gift
came
laugh
·ter·

heart, and i will always pray for you that God will
enable you to do the same."

with God's help, will and i want our little sons to
grow up respecting and loving their birth mothers.
they are as real a part of their lives as we are. both of
them loved their babies so much.

it was painful, both times, for me to say good-bye to
liz and karen. they had carried my babies for me. they
had handed over nine months of work and creation
and sacrifice. i had watched them suffer in giving
birth. we were women with the same kinds of emotions and dreams and fears and insecurities. we had all
been vulnerable, revealing so much of ourselves to
each other. our flaws, our secrets. i wanted goodness
and happiness and every great thing for them. i knew
that by taking their babies, i offered them both great
joy and great sadness.

the day came for karen to leave idaho falls. i pulled up
to the curb of the airport. purposely i had left the
babies at home, not wanting it to be too painful for
karen and wanting us to be able to focus completely
on our good-byes.

"karen, how can will and i ever thank you?"

"ann," karen began, weeping. "oh, ann, it's hard to
give brock up. i love him so much. but ann, he was
yours before i ever delivered him. God used me to
bless you. ann, it's harder for me to give *you* up. how
can i make it through life without you? you are my
dearest friend in the whole world. i am a brand new
Christian. how will i survive without you? i love you
so much. i am so indebted to you and will for loving
brock and raising him to follow God."

and
with
the
gift
came
laugh
·ter·

we sat at the curb and wept. side by side. linked
forever by one small, beautiful creation. liz had
verbalized some of the same sentiments when she left.
we were all bound together by a cord that could
never be broken. by two miracle babies.

"ann, i gave you a son, but you gave me the Son.
i will never be the same."

as she walked into the airport, i buried my face in the
steering wheel and shook with sobs. i had received
another little son and had released another daughter.
i was letting her go, believing with all my heart that
she and God . . . that liz and God . . . would now be
able to do more beautiful, creative, kind things in the
world than ever before.

karen had written me a letter. i didn't move from the
curb until i had read it. i will cherish it forever. before
she left, i had reminded karen again that i wanted her
to meet liz. in many ways they were different—each
unique, special. but they had each had a college
education. they had similar aspirations and dreams of
helping others. and they were bound with a strong
tie—their babies were now brothers. a few weeks
later they did meet on the east coast and became
instant, steadfast friends. now they both live in the
same city and spend many weekends together.

♥ ♥
♥ ♥

taylor likes broccoli and parsley and carrots and celery.

brock spits all that out and begs for popsicles and "canny." both boys look so much like their mothers, especially around their mouths. the way they smile . . . certain expressions. i love seeing those little reminders of liz and karen. i love knowing where those traits and qualities come from.

will and i go to bed every night saying to each other, "what would life be without taylor and brock?" "oh, ann, can you imagine our home without them?"

both will and i put them to bed at night and pray with them . . . will's hands on their heads . . . mine holding their little hands.

"rock me, mommy . . . rock me and sing."

"tell me a story, daddy . . . please."

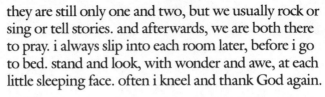

they are still only one and two, but we usually rock or sing or tell stories. and afterwards, we are both there to pray. i always slip into each room later, before i go to bed. stand and look, with wonder and awe, at each little sleeping face. often i kneel and thank God again.

my first trip with brock was when he was four days old. that date had been booked by my agent months before, and karen and i had prayed the baby would come beforehand. i had a week of appearances from pennsylvania to ohio. i was weary after the physical and emotional ordeal karen and i had been through. i had to make sure everything at the office was under control. that will was loved . . . the refrigerator full. then i proceeded to pack for my eleven-month-old . . . my four-day-old . . . and myself.

joyce, taylor's delivery nurse, was going with me. we took two sizes of disposable diapers. plenty of for-mula. bottles for two. the pediatrician checked both babies before we left. will is always a tremendous help . . . he dressed one baby while i dressed the other . . . and we made it to the airport in time for our early morning flight.

on the flight joyce and i passed the babies back and forth, taking turns caring for their needs. while brock was so tiny, i tried to spend most of his sleeping time with taylor. in a way, it seemed tough for taylor, still a baby himself, to be put in a big sibling position. will and i worked very hard at making sure his basic routine didn't change and that he received large doses of love and attention. he traveled very well . . . a regular veteran . . . and brock rarely opened his eyes, except to let us know he was hungry. he was every bit as good-natured as taylor.

on each of our flights, we created something of a scene as the four of us boarded. there was i (size 4)

and
with
the
gift
came
laugh
·ter·

♥

coming aboard with two babies, one of them just a newborn. flight attendants oohed and ahhed.

"they're YOURS?"

"yes. . . ."

"oh, i wish i could have your fabulous figure right after delivery."

joyce and i would smile. "thank you," i'd respond.

sometimes i told them the story . . . sometimes not. sometimes i was just too tired to go into it. and anyway, i enjoyed hearing the raves and just let them soak in!

before i had left home, will had said, "ann, i will let you take brock on this trip with you only if you promise me you will have him circumcised on saturday." obviously, he felt as strongly about it as he had felt about having taylor circumcised on the eighth day. i assured him i would take care of it . . . too overwhelmed with what i had to face the first few days to worry about the fourth day. but i was as aggravated as i could be. how rigid could he be? i thought . . . and begged him to have it done before i left. but no . . . he is very health-oriented, and felt strongly that the traditional, biblical, jewish way was best for brock.

joyce laughed every time i mentioned it to her on the trip. "ann, you have always had so much faith. the way you believe . . . i am just waiting to see if you and God can get this to happen."

"God will do it, joyce. that i am sure. i just don't know how. i am annoyed about it, but there is no doubt in my mind that God will help me because it's so important to will."

and
with
the
gift
came
laugh
·ter·

♥

on saturday . . . brock's eighth day . . . i was speaking in canton, ohio. after a special time with our friends the fishers, in lancaster, pennsylvania, we arrived in canton. i said to the woman who was sponsoring my appearance, "do you know a doctor who can perform a circumcision today?"

"ann," she laughed, "i have brought in many speakers . . . some very important people . . . but never before have i had anyone request a circumcision!"

she got on the phone and began to call every doctor she knew anything about. it was already 2 p.m. (i had meant to call her from one of my other stops, but it had been too difficult to find time.) a couple of times, she had me get on the phone and talk to the doctor myself. one of them agreed to do it at a hospital, but only if i would leave brock there overnight.

"look, mrs. anderson. something might go wrong. he might not stop bleeding. i don't know you or the baby. i can't put myself in a position where i am liable for unforeseen problems."

i knew this wouldn't work. i refused to have my new little baby in a strange hospital overnight. i kept praying . . . begging God to give me some creative idea. my sponsor even tried to find a rabbi who would do it, but was unsuccessful. suddenly i remembered cleora, jan's obstetrician and dear friend in cleveland. that was about an hour away from canton. the big problem was that i had to speak in canton, to a group of six hundred people at a banquet, in only an hour. it was a rather bold, brash thing to call cleora, but i knew she was a remarkable lady, and the worst she could do was to say "no."

i spoke very candidly to her on the phone. "cleora, this is very important to will. he absolutely insists. i have until midnight to get it done. you know he was

and
with
the
gift
came
laugh
·ter·

raised by a father who said there was no excuse for man's failure."

"ann, i would love to. how would it be if i meet you at jan's house at 11:30 p.m.? that gives you time to speak and autograph books, and still be driven to cleveland in time. we'll have thirty minutes to get the job done."

jan was speaking somewhere that night, also, but i reached tom, and he said to come ahead. cleora said she would bring all the equipment herself. joyce just kept shaking her head. it was incredible to her. God's kindness and my persistence had done it.

after i finished speaking at the banquet, i autographed books for forty-five minutes. then some wonderful people drove us to cleveland. i was so exhausted . . . it was amazing that we found tom and jan's house—i was too tired to be of much help. but i was very excited about seeing my family. those three little boys are like my own. when we arrived, jan had barely arrived home from her own speaking engagement. she was shocked to find cleora and two nurses, who had come along as her assistants—labor and delivery nurses who had read my books for years. i was so touched by their kindness in coming to help. it delights and humbles me when i meet people like that.

cleora had the bed-like contraption on the kitchen counter—all the equipment, gloves, and medication used in circumcisions. the younger ream boys were asleep, but tre was wide awake—jan's oldest, who was then eight and a half years old. he wasn't about to go to bed.

"they did that to me once, a long time ago," he said, knowingly, his eyes big. it seemed right for brock's big cousin to witness this historic event.

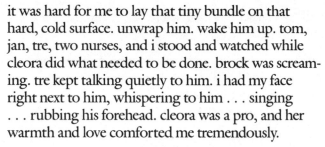

and
with
the
gift
came
laugh
·ter·

♥

it was hard for me to lay that tiny bundle on that
hard, cold surface. unwrap him. wake him up. tom,
jan, tre, two nurses, and i stood and watched while
cleora did what needed to be done. brock was screaming. tre kept talking quietly to him. i had my face
right next to him, whispering to him . . . singing
. . . rubbing his forehead. cleora was a pro, and her
warmth and love comforted me tremendously.

one of the nurses had brought a camera, so not even
brock could ever forget the occasion. tre insisted on
cuddling brock, and carrying him around. i think he
felt brock needed someone to comfort him who
understood things like that. what could a mere
mother know?

cleora had delivered jan's youngest child, and then
circumcised brock, so now she is a member of our
family for life. i know of no other doctor and nurses
who would have been so selfless and kind as those
three. when the clock struck midnight, brock was still
whimpering, but the job was done. i gave him some
medication, then fell into bed, with my arm around
him all night.

before brock was sixteen months old, karen got to see
him three times, just as liz had seen taylor. after
leaving idaho falls, she had flown to dallas to visit
some friends for a few weeks. during that time i was
asked by a leading infertility specialist in the dallas
area to speak about my own struggles. it was an
overnight trip, so we decided to leave taylor with
lindsey, his little friend, and just take brock—three
weeks old—for karen to see.

that night, in an auditorium, will and i both shared
our experiences with many couples who were having
similar sorrows. karen and her sister were in the

and
with
the
gift
came
laugh
·ter·

audience. again, people were overwhelmed by the love and closeness we seemed to share. she and her sister visited with us in the hotel room afterwards. she was so undemanding, just as liz had been. so willing to fit in and be happy with any time we had.

on another occasion, i called her. "i'll be coming through your city in a few days and will have a one-hour layover in the airport. would you like to spend that time with brock and me? taylor isn't coming until the next day, with the nurse. we could have a wonderful visit and you could see brock at eight months, if you would like."

"oh, ann, i'd love to! can i really?"

i dressed brock in his most darling outfit . . . combed his curly hair perfectly. we walked off the plane, and there was karen with homemade cookies for me and a toy for brock. we hugged, and shed a few tears. i suggested we go to one of the airport restaurants not far from the gate. we sat and talked and laughed and visited, frequently passing brock back and forth across the table. a striking-looking couple, with a little girl, sat down next to us. once, when the woman caught my eye, she asked me, "is he your baby?"

"yes." i smiled. karen and i exchanged a secret wink.

"he's absolutely beautiful!"

suddenly i realized it would soon be time to board my next flight. karen and brock and i started out of the coffee shop, but then i turned to karen. "i just feel we should go back and tell that couple the real story."

"ann! i would be terrified," karen said, smiling and frowning at the same time. "they were so impressive. i am way too shy to talk to them."

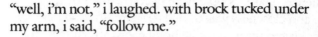

and
with
the
gift
came
laugh
·ter·

♥

"well, i'm not," i laughed. with brock tucked under my arm, i said, "follow me."

"excuse me," i said, sitting right next to the woman. "my name is ann. this is karen. i have a plane to catch, but i just have to tell you our story, if i may. i am the adoptive mother. she is the birth mother. in a way, this baby belongs to both of us."

the woman's eyes were warm . . . and moist. she gazed at me steadily.

"about five weeks before he was born, i lost a set of twins, and my husband and i were heartbroken. we were in the delivery room when this little boy was born. we really believe that God sometimes takes . . . and sometimes gives . . . and whatever He does, it is good. i love this young woman, and i love my baby so much."

the couple stared at us in awe. we all had tears in our eyes. karen sat there . . . so beautiful . . . so radiant.

"i have another beautiful little boy, eleven months older, with another amazing story. i just wanted you to know."

they thanked us profusely. karen and i ran to the gate. i handed brock to her for one more hug and kiss. we embraced . . . and our tears were only of joy and wonder.

our last meeting was when brock was sixteen months old. jan and her baby, and i with my two were passing through the same airport. it seemed important to me that karen and liz have equal experiences and opportunities, if possible. jan and i were on our way to appear on television. a one-hour layover. it was the day before our birthday.

and
with
the
gift
came
laugh
·ter·

karen had baked us a scrumptious carrot cake, and she brought the little boys a real red football. she loved watching taylor and brock together . . . seeing brock's growth. the boys loved the football and we all had bites of cake. it was another memorable encounter. it would be the last one until brock is grown up. last hugs and thanks . . . and some tears. my next letter from karen assured me that they had not been tears of sadness or regret on her part, but of much love and gratitude to God. and my tears were for love of karen, for my two babies, for God's plans that are so much better than ours could ever be.

will and i could not have produced two more wonderful babies. every loss seems insignificant when we think of them. we really believe that someday we will meet our unborn babies in heaven. but we are so glad that God saved taylor and brock for us. they have brought us sunshine, rainbows, starlight, sunset— beauty in our lives.

people often ask us if the babies have affected our marriage. have children caused problems? will and i shake our heads and laugh. problems? they have made us a family. they have given us reasons for ice-cream cones and popcorn parties and shopping in toy departments. for a house filled with animated conversations about child-rearing and discipline. new, fun trips and projects for all of us. they have allowed will and me to love each other so much more because we now understand so much more about love. their presence makes that love exceptional . . . complete. the babies force us to reach into our deepest places and find new or once-hidden corners full of love and warmth. they have brought God closer to us through their utter simplicity and innocence and vulnerability. they make Christmas come alive. and thanksgiving

and
with
the
gift
came
laugh
·ter·

♥

something to celebrate. on halloween i stood on the front porch and watched taylor dressed as a dinosaur and brock as a little girl, with his hair pulled up in a bow. the little neighborhood girls were with them. they were so happy and excited as the girls dragged them from house to house, almost faster than their legs could carry them. cheeks rosy from the cold.

they have enhanced our marriage and our lives in every way. love dances down the halls and sits at our dinner table, and we say, "alleluia. alleluia! amen."

♥ ♥
♥ ♥

"ann,
i have to go to europe
for three and a half
weeks in june,
and i want you and
the babies to go too,"
will casually commented, one
evening at dinner.

"oh, will . . . ! honey, that's on the
other side of the world! will they
have plenty of disposable diapers?
maybe the hotels won't be
equipped for babies. taylor will be
barely two and brock just past one.
no, you go on. i really feel great
about your business prospects
there, but i think the babies and i
should stay here."

but will persisted . . . he brought
it up frequently. four of his business associates, with their wives
and children, were going to go.
he wanted me to get to know

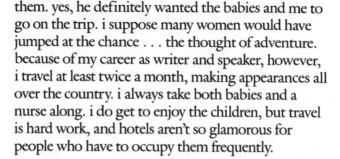

and
with
the
gift
came
laugh
·ter·

♥

them. yes, he definitely wanted the babies and me to
go on the trip. i suppose many women would have
jumped at the chance . . . the thought of adventure.
because of my career as writer and speaker, however,
i travel at least twice a month, making appearances all
over the country. i always take both babies and a
nurse along. i do get to enjoy the children, but travel
is hard work, and hotels aren't so glamorous for
people who have to occupy them frequently.

when will and i have a major decision to make, and if
we cannot come to a complete agreement, i always
submit to him. he kept reassuring me about details of
the trip—he said it would be easy to take boxes of
diapers along . . . that the men had agreed to hire two
full-time nannies to help with all the children in the
group (there would be two other small ones besides
taylor and brock) . . . that the hotels would be the
best. i still had some misgivings—partly because of
the chernobyl disaster that had recently happened—
but i agreed to get ready. i still thought of it as an
ordeal, and i think that a part of me still hoped that
God would close the door, even though i wanted to
submit to will!

we talked about how much fun it would be to have
someone i knew and loved to join us. i had not yet
met the other men's families, and with will occupied
with business every day, i thought it would be special
to have someone with us whom i especially enjoyed.
our dear friends paul and margaret had gone around
the world with us several years before, and we had
had a wonderful time—but they had a wedding to
attend in june. we would have loved to have tom and
jan, but they had other obligations.

"honey, how about joanne? she has her own business.
maybe she can make some contacts there, too."

and
with
the
gift
came
laugh
·ter·

♥

will was ecstatic . . . he loves joanne as much as i do.
she is one of my favorite people in the world. from
boston. has five grown children. beautiful, exciting,
authentic . . . and God's. she had gone with me on
my first trip to israel, and we had traveled a lot
together. i don't know anyone who does not get
along with joanne and love her. she would add
pizzazz to the whole group!

when we called her, she was amazed to hear the dates
of the trip . . . those were days her store would be
closed for some repairs. she was free . . . she would
join us. will and i were both thrilled.

vaccinations. passports for the babies. three huge
boxes of disposable diapers. medicine from the
pediatrician to help the boys sleep during part of the
long overseas flight. my clothes and the babies'
organized and packed. everything arranged with my
secretary and agent to cover office details while i was
away. lomotil in case we had diarrhea. many reassur-
ances to my family that God would take care of us.
we were ready. there seemed to be no "nos," only
"yeses."

our flight out of idaho falls was to leave at 7:35 a.m.
although i use that flight frequently, i never find it
easy to get showered and shampooed . . . two babies
ready . . . and to the airport for that departure. will
loaded the car . . . strapped the babies in. i picked up
the last few stray toys and put them into the nursery.
(i was raised by a mother who always left our house
spotless before we left on vacations. if anything
should happen to us while we were gone, she didn't
want anyone to think her a poor housekeeper. i must
have learned that from her!)

we arrived at the airport at 7:25 a.m., ten minutes

and
with
the
gift
came
laugh
·ter·

♥

early. like most people who fly all the time, we like to get there just in time to board.

"mr. anderson, you and your wife tend to cut it too close. i am sorry, but we have already boarded standby passengers in your seats," announced the ticket agent at our small airport. i stood there with my mouth open. it seemed just too incredible.

will, very much in charge and calmly assertive, said, "listen, one or the other of us flies out of this airport at least once every two weeks. you know us. it is not legal to put standbys in our seats ten minutes before departure."

"i'm sorry, mr. anderson, but we are not going to unload them now. you will just have to learn to organize your time better. . . ."

still unable to move . . . brock in my arms and taylor at my side . . . with all our luggage and diaper boxes around me . . . i stared in disbelief.

"ann and i are on our way to europe, sir," will persisted quietly. "this flight helps us make all our connections . . . even to meeting our traveling companions in new york and flying overseas with them." then, finally realizing that the man wasn't going to budge, will whirled around, grabbed three or four pieces of luggage, and commanded, "ann, get the babies into the car. quickly!"

i ran out and buckled them in, too weak to help will load everything back into the trunk. jumping in, will behind the wheel, we whipped our clean new car out of the parking place and across grass and dirt, through the weeds, and under a wire of some sort, and pulled up in front of the private airport, which serves small aircraft.

and
with
the
gift
came
laugh
·ter·

♥

"what is your fastest plane? i mean, the very fastest plane on the lot. i have to get my family to salt lake city in thirty minutes to make a connection to new york."

"well, uh, sir . . . our fastest plane is, uh, very expensive to charter . . . ," the man in the blue jumpsuit stammered.

"money is not an issue. get it. i want it. immediately," will ordered, slapping a credit card on the counter.

i stood there, thinking, "maybe this is God's 'no.' maybe we aren't supposed to go after all. maybe i was right. maybe our plane will be hijacked by terrorists." sort of whimpering, i said to will, "will, honey, don't you think this might be God's way of saying 'no'?"

will looked exasperated. "ann, i know God wants us to go!"

several men ran out and grabbed our things out of the trunk. i hung on to both babies while will signed papers, arranged for one of the men to park the car, and guided me to the rather large, fancy-looking aircraft. i shuddered to think how much this was costing . . . but will was paying the bills, so why should i be worried about it?

will had the pilot call ahead to make sure that the rest of our reservations had not been cancelled when we missed our first flight. when we landed in salt lake city, a van was waiting and it whisked us away to the main terminal. running through the terminal and around the corners, we arrived at our gate about twenty minutes before the flight was to leave. will stood in line. when he finally reached the desk, the agent said, "oh, i'm sorry, sir. i show no reservations for you and mrs. anderson and two infants. anyway,

and
with
the
gift
came
laugh
·ter·

♥

we have twenty standbys ahead of you, and there is no way whatsoever that you can make this flight."

again, i stood there frozen . . . hanging on to two tired babies who had been swept out of their beds at 5:30 a.m. i felt awful, but i couldn't tell whether i was beginning to feel sick because i was so upset by all of this confusion, or because i really had something wrong with me.

once more i asked will, weakly, "honey, doesn't this mean anything to you? don't you believe God is shouting, 'NO'?"

"no, ann. absolutely not. i know it is right for us to go," he said quietly but firmly. my eyes filled with tears. he put his arm around me and hugged me. "honey, the next flight to kennedy airport is in seven hours. let's call bill and penny and we'll have some fun while we wait." bill and penny are our close friends in salt lake city . . . the ones we named brock after. picking taylor up, i followed will and brock to the horizon club.

when we finally arrived at new york kennedy airport hours later, it was after midnight. will dragged all the luggage to an airport bus that dropped us at the hotel not far away.

we had missed our friends, of course. i had no idea what had happened to joanne . . . i knew she wouldn't recognize the others in the party. they were all enroute from chicago, while we were having our various problems, so there was no way for any of us to connect with the others.

will always takes such good care of the babies and me . . . hustling the bags around . . . getting porters . . . soothing me with a smile and a pat . . . carrying one of the babies with him. the next morning he

i have
a few
quiet,
reflective
moments

baby's
dresser
with gifts
from
so many
who
celebrated
too

♥♥
♥♥

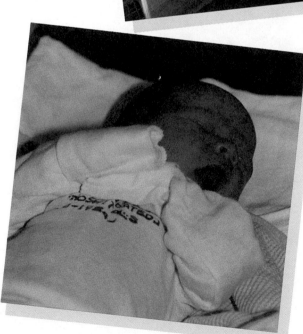

taylor
jenkins
anderson,
at
birth

with
our
obstetrician,
dr. jim,
the day
we
brought
brock
home

will
holding
two-
day-
old
brock

taylor
at
nine
months

taylor's
second
easter;
hunting
for
eggs
at
grandma
jo's
house

taylor
and
brock—
"getting
to
know
you"

♥♥
♥♥

all
dressed
up
and
really
going
places

with
brock
at
expo '86
in
vancouver,
b.c.

brock,
very
much
at home
in
airports,
even
at age
one

will
and
taylor
(practicing
to be
a new
england
patriot?)

taylor
with
a teddy
bear
friend . . .
sent by
prisoners
on
death
row

♥♥
♥♥

the
boys
loved
their
helicopter
ride

on
our
trip
abroad,
june
1986

we
love
reading
books!

♥ ♥
♥ ♥

time
out to
cuddle
and
talk
things
over

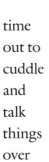

 taylor
and
brock,
2½
and 1½

will,
taylor,
and
brock

go
fishing

at our
house,
everybody
loves
ice-
cream
cones!

♥ ♥
♥ ♥

Christmas
1986.
special
days
mean
so much
more
now

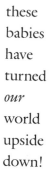

these
babies
have
turned
our
world
upside
down!

jan and i always dreamed of being mothers. here are the five sons God has given us: tre, brock, christian, taylor, and nash

brock and i visit grandma kiemel in honolulu

with friends in florida on taylor's second birthday

taylor
and i,
with
aunt jan
and
cousin
christian

brock
and
taylor
adore
grandma
jo

our
little
friend
seanne
(left, front)
and her
newborn
baby
sister,
charissa

dr.
kenneth n.
taylor
with his
namesake.
how
we hope
our sons
will have
dr. taylor's
love for
God's Word

♥♥
♥♥

taylor
with
glenn
jenkins,
from
whom
he got
his
middle
name

and
with
the
gift
came
laugh
·ter·

♥

would have to put the pieces together, and we'd try to catch the same flight to our destination.

our hotel room was beautiful . . . clean . . . new . . . cool. i felt so happy and secure with will and the two babies, all safe and together.

taylor and brock are such fabulous babies. so good-natured and easygoing. so used to airplanes and hotels . . . otherwise we could never survive ordeals like this one. i crawled between the clean sheets, with the little boys snuggled between will and me, and just died. everything seemed insignificant to me except sleep!

will was up early, phoning, arranging, connecting. we went downstairs for a late breakfast, but i just didn't feel like eating. in fact, i felt horrible, but i could not bear to tell will, for he had kept so calm and cheerful through all this. how could i lay one more burden on him?

the bellman had come to get our bags in preparation for our going to the airport, when will put his arms around me, telling me what a trouper i had been and how much he appreciated it. "ann!" he stepped back, startled, and felt my face. "you are burning up! you're sick!"

i burst into tears and said, "i know . . . i just couldn't bear to tell you. you have had so many problems, and you are so determined to go on this trip."

"well, we are not going *anywhere* until you are better!"

he excused the bellman and told me he was going out but would be back in a few minutes. the babies were playing with little bars of soap . . . and the telephone. i lay huddled on the bed. thirty minutes later will returned with two thermometers. he had taken a cab and they had had to drive miles and miles to find a

and
with
the
gift
came
laugh
·ter·

♥

drugstore and to investigate about a doctor at kennedy airport. my fever was very high. we took the
babies, crawled into another cab, and went to the
airport "dispensary." all the nurses and doctors were
foreign, with almost unintelligible accents. the little
examining room looked like something from a
saturday evening post cover. after some tests, the
doctor announced i had a kidney infection. he pre-
scribed an antibiotic, and the four of us straggled out
of the little tiny room, and waited thirty minutes for a
cab to take us back to the hotel.

"ann, we won't leave this country until you are well.
i am not about to take you across the world sick. i feel
very relaxed about the delay . . . we will just stay here.
i will take care of taylor and brock, and you rest."

i lifted my aching head off the pillow and pushed the
hair out of my eyes. i moaned, "oh, honey, aren't you
even worried about the money?"

"money? absolutely not! now lie down."

within twenty-four hours my fever had broken, and
two days later we were on our way. everything had
started off so badly that i feared we were embarking
on the greatest fiasco of our lives, but i knew there
was no turning back.

our friend joanne had waited and waited for us in the
boarding area. she is an experienced world traveler,
but this would be quite a venture, especially since she
did not even know the name of the hotel where we
would be staying. she picked up her carry-on luggage
and boarded the plane. as she walked toward her seat,
she heard a man say something that made her realize
instinctively he was one of our group.

"pardon me, but are you looking for will anderson
too?"

and
with
the
gift
came
laugh
·ter·
♥

steve, one of will's associates, said, "yes! and i'll bet you are joanne!"

when we finally caught up with our group, taylor and brock—who had been absolutely perfect through the whole trip—clapped their hands and seemed as happy and relieved as we were. bob met us at the airport and drove us back to the hotel in one of the two vans they had rented.

i stood there amazed and surveyed the gorgeous hotel lobby. it was as elegant and beautiful as the finest hotel in america. bob and alice, gary and joanna, steve and helen, and joanne were all there to greet us. i felt wonderful . . . exhilarated.

we were introduced to the two young women who had been hired as nannies. both spoke english, which was, of course, very important. one of them looked at me, wide-eyed with awe. she whispered, "are you ann kiemel, the lady who writes books?"

"yes!" i smiled, excited.

we slipped into our hotel room and she told me the most remarkable story. "ann, my father is a professor. i grew up believing man is everything. and science. one day my friend and i were standing on a street corner. 'see those people over there?' my friend asked. 'they are Christians. they believe in God; can you imagine that?' and ann, i really could not conceive of anyone's believing in God. so i marched across the street and confronted them. 'how can you believe in God? are you crazy? do you not understand science?'

"a young man looked at me, ann, and quietly asked if he could tell me his story. he was a visitor to our country. as he spoke, i felt my heart melting. i had no control over it. what he said was the truth . . . i knew

and
with
the
gift
came
laugh
·ter·

♥

it. i received Jesus as my personal Savior that day. my family and friends rejected me. i felt very much alone. all i had was the little Bible he gave me . . . and God himself. about a year and a half ago, a woman from america sent me your book *yes*. i had been about ready to forsake God, not because i did not love him and believe, but because i could not stand the pain of such loneliness any longer.

"i sat down and began to read your simple little book. 'yes' to loneliness. to pain. to singleness. 'yes' to God. i decided that if you could say 'yes,' i could too. my life will never be the same. i can't believe i am really meeting you!"

all those weeks i had tried to talk will out of my coming, with the babies, on this trip . . . even to the very last difficult days. now i stood in awe of the way God had worked . . . he had placed this young woman as one of the two nannies, knowing that she and i had been friends already through my book. knowing she needed me. for three and a half weeks those two girls traveled everywhere with us. stayed in our hotels. flew with us. for many hours i laughed and shared with them . . . enjoying them. we prayed together in private. and all the children (six in all) loved them. they took special care of taylor and brock, because they were so young and because i was the mother with two babies.

every night, while the children played at the hotel and were bathed and tucked into bed, the adults went to wonderful little places for dinner. the food was superb. we took walks beside a lake on moonlit evenings. we sunned by the swimming pools and on the beaches. we had times of singing and sharing in our rooms.

and
with
the
gift
came
laugh
·ter·

one afternoon joanne and i put the babies down for
naps and left them in the care of the nannies. then we
found our way to the elegant dining room, where a
waiter served us, one dish at a time, from the buffet.
there was fine linen, crystal, sterling silver. all around
us were people from all over the world. we were so
busy watching the people, we could hardly eat the
delicious food. soon will and some others of our
group joined us. we enjoyed laughter, warmth, and
the excitement of being in a faraway world, caught up
in a magical kaleidoscope of color. traveling to new
places. breathing different air . . . walking new
sidewalks . . . all this gives a rich, fresh quality to life.

will and i would stroll to the parks with our babies
and let them dip their toes in the ponds and watch the
birds, sometimes chasing them. often will would take
turns hoisting first taylor, and then brock, to his
shoulders so they could see farther and feel stronger
and taller than the rest of us.

i had always loved joanne. now i love her even more.
we have so much more deposited in our memory
banks to share. some days she accompanied the men
in their business negotiations. at other times she and i
would go shopping. the rest of the group became like
family to me. we laughed together . . . once in awhile
one of us shed some tears, but we stuck together. our
children looked after each other.

one evening we took taylor and brock with us to
dinner. we did this occasionally, so we could share the
evening with them . . . and help them learn the good
manners of dining out . . . and just for fun. by the
time we returned to the hotel, it was 11 p.m. although
we had a beautiful, large room, the management had
been able to find only one baby bed for us, so the

and
with
the
gift
came
laugh
·ter·

boys took turns sleeping in it, while the other one
would sleep with will and me.

will decided that it was brock's turn to sleep with us
and taylor's turn to be in the crib.

"mommy," taylor whined, "i want to sleep in the big
bed."

i was tired, and it was late. i didn't care if they both
slept with us. why make an issue out of anything that
late at night? that was my philosophy. anyway—
though i believe in being fair about taking turns—i
didn't think it mattered either way to brock, so why
not just stick taylor in our bed and all get to sleep?

"now, taylor, daddy loves you very much . . . but it is
late. it is your turn to sleep in the crib. if you keep
crying, i will just have to spank you."

i cringed. oh, please, i thought . . . please . . . let's not
have discipline tonight. will plopped little brock next
to me, and i nestled him under my arm. taylor continued to cry, so will proceeded to get the wooden
spoon that we always use for spankings. (oh, yes, we
had brought it with us, all the way to europe!) quietly
he lifted taylor out of the crib, set him on his lap, and
explained it all to him. then turned him over and
spanked him. i slipped out of bed and went into the
bathroom. closing the door, i buried my face in my
hands and cried. will is such a consistent, loving, fun
father. i knew taylor should be held accountable after
several warnings. but i was a mother. softer. i could
hardly stand it, yet i knew supporting will was more
important than protecting taylor's bottom. so i did
my crying in secret.

will wiped taylor's nose, gave him a drink, and laid
him back in bed. tucked him in. "daddy loves you.

and
with
the
gift
came
laugh
·ter·

tomorrow night it will be your turn." meanwhile,
brock was sitting up in our bed and jabbering
nonstop. "mama . . . dada . . . goo goo." will walked
over and picked up his one-year-old. "brock, see this
spoon? daddy doesn't want to have to spank you too.
but if you do not go to sleep, i will. put your head
down and close your eyes. it's late."

he placed brock down beside me again, and i heaved a
sigh of relief. ("oh, please, dear God, help brock not
to get spanked too. i don't think i can stand it twice.")
for five minutes, brock lay perfectly still. taylor did
not make a peep. i was just beginning to relax and fall
asleep, when brock shot his head up and began his
gibberish again.

will popped up, picked brock up, got the spoon,
explained it all, and turned him over his knee. *whack.*
whack. whack. with big eyes, taylor watched from his
bed. brock yelled, sobbed. then the same procedure
. . . "i love you, brock, very, very much." tight hugs
. . . pats . . . nose wiping . . . cold drink. will laid him
at the other end of taylor's bed, covering them both
with the same blanket. lights out.

for thirty minutes, whispering in the dark, will and i
discussed this whole experience. shared our feelings.
talked it over. i know it had been harder on me than
on the babies. they slept soundly all night and
awakened so happy. so delighted with daddy and
daylight and life in general. it was the last time . . . the
only time on the whole trip . . . they had to be disciplined about going to sleep.

on the flight home, i turned to will. "honey, you
know why i married you? for adventure, that's why!
darling, thank you for this memory!" our children
had added so much to the memory. and happy

and
with
the
gift
came
laugh
·ter·

♥

memories are such an important key to their wholeness and joy. taylor still talks about the trip . . . about
slipping in the swimming pool and being "rescued."
brock took his very first steps while in our hotel
room . . . the nannies had worked with him, coaxing
him constantly. there were many tears when they said
good-bye to the babies.

taylor and brock will not remember all of it as they
grow, but the pictures are in the album, and the
stories live. we are building family history for them
. . . hours of future storytelling. they are learning to
be happy anywhere. to sleep in any bed. to be resilient.
to like people. to be more whole.

i know that most children can't go to faraway places.
and we may never get that opportunity again. most
great memories come from simple plans. when i was a
little girl, my parents rented a tiny cottage on the
other side of oahu. just a few steps from the ocean. a
little gas stove in the kitchen . . . mother baked little
cakes and muffins for us. at night we swam in the
dark, giggling, close together. we drove to waikiki
and parked by a sidewalk . . . years ago, before traffic
and tourists made it impossible. we would sit for two
hours, jan and i in the backseat, just watching people.

the house we lived in was a "parsonage." so plain and
ordinary, except for my mother's special touches. the
car we drove . . . always an older model. my father's
salary . . . very modest. but no one can take away the
bedtime stories. the homemade cakes for supper. the
overnight vacations twenty miles away.

will and i do not spend our money on a lot of material
possessions. we give God his share first, and then we
spend money to create memories for our children and
others we love. those are the only things no one can

take away. when health is gone . . . or someone dies
. . . or it's a hard year at school, the memories are still
there—to open the windows of a child's mind . . . to
make him laugh and feel warm and strong inside,
where it counts.

♥ ♥
♥ ♥

through a miraculous chain of events,

will and i, with the babies and joanne, were able to travel home by way of frankfurt for a weekend, and then to the U.S. without having to pay extra fare. this gave us an opportunity to see clark and ann, our dear friends in germany. they have a little girl, seanne, three and a half. they have tried unsuccessfully to bring another baby into the world.

as we were leaving germany, i said to them, "clark and ann, i feel a strong conviction that God is going to give you another baby."

about three days after we arrived home, our phone rang one morning. it was my friend mary. "ann, do you know of anyone special who is waiting for a baby? i have a lovely young woman who will

and
with
the
gift
came
laugh
·ter·
♥

deliver in about two months, and she wants to talk to you."

"mary, i have the perfect family! i would love to talk to the girl."

her name isn't really dawn, but that's what we'll call her. she was petite and pretty, with dark hair. eighteen years old. she already had one darling little girl, a year and a half old. this pregnancy was from a different father—"devin," seventeen years old. i met him, too . . . very attractive boy with fine features. still in school. they had agreed it was best for the baby to give it up. again, a painful decision. a decision made because of deep love and concern for the baby and a longing to do for it what they would never be able to do.

when we contacted clark and ann, they were ecstatic. it was the answer to many prayers. they would return to america in time to meet dawn and devin before the birth. they arrived at our house a week before the due date, bringing little nighties and blankets. a tremendous sense of excitement permeated our home . . . but we had our three toddlers (aged one, two, and three and a half) to bring us down to earth . . . to face reality frequently.

about a month before their arrival, i had been asked to speak for the pregnancy hotline in idaho falls. usually i do not make local appearances, but this cause was close to my heart, so i agreed. the auditorium was quite full, and a tender, warm spirit seemed to surround us. afterwards, one of the women who work for the hotline mentioned to me that she would like to bring a pregnant girl to see me. a girl who had called the hotline. the counselor had taken her to a local counseling agency, but the girl wasn't comfortable there. could i work with her?

and
with
the
gift
came
laugh
·ter·

i feel a special connection and love for unwed mothers. two of them have made me a mother, and i am gratefully indebted forever. i cannot fully understand their emotions, but i do know what loss is, and i do understand what it means to receive a baby in this way.

carrie (also a fictitious name) was lovely . . . pretty . . . her husband in prison for at least five more years. she also had a baby about a year and a half old. she, too, wanted her baby to be loved . . . to have a really solid Christian home. and she, too, struggled with having to part with a piece of herself that she had grown to love. looking through my letters, i found a couple   david and linda—from a south dakota farm, who had been married eleven years and had lost eight babies through miscarriages. i let carrie call them; she talked to linda on the phone and said she sounded "really sweet."

as with dawn, i wanted carrie to think about it for a few days. to be sure she felt good, deep inside, about her choice. she met me at my office the next week and told me she felt great about this family. it sounded wonderful to her for her baby to grow up on a farm. she had talked to her husband, in prison, and he was very supportive.

i spent hours with both of these girls . . . talking with them about all their options . . . making sure they really felt at peace about their decisions . . . letting them tell me all the myriad of feelings. dawn's mother lived nearby, as did her father, who was now married to someone else. will and i met with her father and stepmother, and also with her mother and stepfather. the entire family loved dawn very much and agreed that she had made the best decision for herself and the baby.

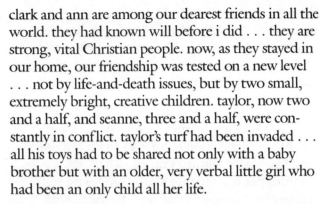

and
with
the
gift
came
laugh
·ter·

♥

clark and ann are among our dearest friends in all the
world. they had known will before i did . . . they are
strong, vital Christian people. now, as they stayed in
our home, our friendship was tested on a new level
. . . not by life-and-death issues, but by two small,
extremely bright, creative children. taylor, now two
and a half, and seanne, three and a half, were constantly in conflict. taylor's turf had been invaded . . .
all his toys had to be shared not only with a baby
brother but with an older, very verbal little girl who
had been an only child all her life.

we two couples had formulated somewhat different
philosophies of child-rearing. will and i were very
relaxed, casual. we left our children at home and had
dinner out together once a week—just the two of us.
the babies had stayed with nurses in hotel rooms,
while i spoke, since they were newborns. they had
been with crowds of people, either on stage or afterwards, while i autographed books. they were always
happy to have a neighbor girl come to stay with
them . . . they knew we would be back in a couple of
hours.

we keep a wooden spoon on top of our refrigerator.
both taylor and brock know what it is for. we try very
hard to give them plenty of room to be human and
imperfect, but we work at being consistent, and we
punish when we need to. after one of the boys has to
be spanked, he gets lots of hugs and a cold drink.
then he gets to carry the spoon and put it back on top
of the refrigerator as one of us lifts him up.

seanne is darling . . . very feminine . . . and she had a
couple of traits that i think of as being particularly
common with girls—whining and tattling. taylor's
problem was that he was too confident and aggres-
sive, and he would push her down or hit her if she

and
with
the
gift
came
laugh
·ter·

♥

bothered him. both children were intellectually advanced, so they were pretty evenly matched there.

whenever taylor did something that wasn't just right, seanne reported it. many times i got the spoon down and marched him into the bedroom for a spanking. seanne would listen and watch.

it is amazing how relatively detached and impersonal adults can be when discussing politics or war or economics, or even spiritual values. the four of us had much fun together . . . we loved good food and ice cream . . . and discussing great ideas. we could all be termed dreamers. ann is one of the most honest, transparent, affirming people i know . . . and one of the most beautiful. and clark just radiates depth and character. but we had two squabbling toddlers in our midst, and it was hard not to become defensive, angry, confused, resentful. . . . each couple wanting to protect its child . . . feeling partial to him or her in each conflict.

one night, when the children were all in bed, the adults were sitting in the living room . . . tension pervaded the atmosphere. suddenly will cleared his throat and said, "i feel angry! in two weeks, while we have been waiting for this baby, taylor has had at least twenty spankings, and seanne has had none. look, it takes two to tangle, and this situation is just not right."

we began to talk . . . to lay all our feelings on the table. we verbalized our hurt . . . our stress . . . two families living in one house with three tiny children . . . with the great emotional pull and excitement of waiting for dawn's baby to arrive . . . and the uncertainties of the adoption process. clark and ann were so real. they talked about how much they were

and
with
the
gift
came
laugh
·ter·

learning from us . . . how amazed they were at the deep sense of security our babies displayed. they were excited because they had started leaving seanne at home with our babies, and they had watched her learn to feel okay about that. they were surprised at how happy our sons seem to be to go to their cribs at night . . . how much they usually love bedtime. they had started putting seanne down after storytime and prayers and expecting her to go to sleep by herself.

"you know, i believe seanne bugs taylor . . . pushes him over the brink . . . and then enjoys seeing him get a spanking," clark confessed honestly.

"what do you think we should do?" ann asked, very open and earnest.

"the next time the two of them get into a serious conflict, they should both get spanked, no matter who started it," will answered. "and i will spank both of them, if you want me to. if they know they will both get spanked, it will give them both an incentive to get along. my dad did this with my sisters, chris and julie, and me when we were little, and it worked miracles."

we all laughed . . . the tension eased.

"i completely agree with your idea," clark said. "and i will handle seanne!"

the next morning we explained it very clearly to seanne and taylor. when the first fracas developed, clark marched seanne off to their room. will took taylor to ours. screams and wails came from both rooms, while ann and i just smiled at each other nervously.

what a difference that made! immediately the mood began to change. they really worked on their relation-

and
with
the
gift
came
laugh
·ter·

♥

ship. seanne hated spankings more than anything, and we saw a tremendous change in her. the tone of her voice changed . . . her whining began to subside. she and taylor had a few skirmishes, but in general, peace returned! for weeks after they left, taylor missed seanne and wanted to know when we could go to her house. it seemed to us that he taught her to be more assertive . . . to stand up for herself. she taught him so much about playing make-believe . . . a creative imagination.

dawn was overdue. i was scheduled to speak at a large convention in milwaukee. although i had been sort of the central figure in the relationship between dawn and devin and clark and ann, we all felt that the doctor should not induce labor just so i could be present. i had everything arranged . . . the attorney notified . . . the details planned for them to follow if i was on the road when the baby came.

carrie's baby, though due later, arrived two weeks early. i was with her briefly in labor. sheila and eileen, tremendous women who worked with the pregnancy hotline, were with her during her delivery. she produced a beauty . . . a 9-pound, 10½-ounce baby girl with lots of dark hair. a darling baby. i raced over to the hospital to see her and to make sure she still wanted david and linda to have the baby.

there is something indescribable about a girl who has just delivered . . . tired, weak, no makeup . . . but she has a radiance, a natural beauty, an aura of warmth and peace. nine long months of responsibility carried out, climaxed by the agony of giving birth . . . a great mission completed.

david and linda were elated to hear the news and were on a plane within hours. carrie washed her hair and

and
with
the
gift
came
laugh
·ter·

♥

put on makeup . . . wore a new nightie . . . dressed
the baby in special, pretty little things she had prepared, with a lovely hand-knitted baby blanket. her
desire was to hand the baby girl to her new mother
and father.

no couple could have seemed more perfect for this
baby than david and linda. i will never forget the
sense of love and strength they projected. they were
solid. we stood around carrie's bed . . . cried . . . sang
. . . prayed together. carrie had signed the release
papers earlier. now, in a sacred moment, she kissed
the baby one more time and then handed them
rebecca ann (the name they had chosen) and said,
"here's your little girl."

linda held the baby next to her, stroking her cheeks
with one finger. "we cannot express how thankful we
are," said david in a husky voice. "we promise to teach
her about Jesus and his love. i picture her sitting on
the piano bench, next to linda, learning lots of songs.
and she can play with the animals."

"we really love her," linda choked, finding it hard to
talk.

down the hall and into the elevator we went. ann and
little seanne had come along . . . it was a rehearsal for
them . . . a prelude. they were in awe. linda stood in
the elevator, tears flowing uncontrollably, gazing at
rebecca. "i just cannot believe i really have a baby. she
is really ours!"

the look on her face is something i will never forget.
i held the baby for a few minutes . . . kissed her . . .
prayed over her . . . and handed her back. seanne
kissed her on the forehead, and we told them good-
night. they spent the night in a local hotel, then flew
back to south dakota the next morning. carrie left the

and
with
the
gift
came
laugh
·ter·

♥

hospital the next day, and sheila and eileen stuck very close to her.

today, carrie is maturing beautifully. she is working part-time and spending the rest of her time with her little son. she seems so at peace with her decision. every time she talks about david and linda or rebecca, she speaks with enthusiasm and joy. it seems to make her happy to know God has used her to bless a couple so profoundly. she had always wanted a little girl, and she and her husband hope that someday they will have one when the time is right.

when rebecca was one month old, linda wrote and sent a picture of her. and david wrote too, expressing unbelievable joy and pride over the baby. "i never knew adopting a baby could be such a wonderful thing. we cannot imagine loving a baby of our own flesh more than we love rebecca." and how deeply will and i understand and relate to that!

a few days later i flew, with taylor and brock, to milwaukee . . . and dawn went into labor. after addressing several thousand women and signing dozens of books, i fell into bed (taylor and brock asleep in the king-sized bed beside me) and called idaho . . . the maternity floor of the hospital. (i was becoming very familiar with the labor and delivery nurses!) my dear friend joyce answered.

"this is ann anderson. has dawn had her baby?"

"yes, a little girl, ann. five pounds . . . very cute little baby. would you like to talk to dawn? she's in recovery, but i'll move her bed over here by the phone."

it had all happened without me and had gone smoothly. dawn's beautiful young mother (my age) had been with her, and clark and ann were waiting in the little room next door.

and
with
the
gift
came
laugh
·ter·

"dawn, this is ann. how are you? what are you feeling?"

we talked as best friends. we had walked down this
road together. she was like my own child . . . i cared
so much for her.

"it's going to be hard, ann. harder because it's a
girl . . . and because i have stevie, i know what i will
be missing. but i still know it's right."

devin, the young father, was with her. dawn put him
on the phone. he was in tears . . . it had been pretty
overwhelming for him to watch the girl he loved go
through such stress and pain. and then to see his very
own flesh-and-blood creation. he had walked into the
hospital a boy; he would walk out a man, having seen
in vivid technicolor the weight of accountability for
one's behavior. clark and ann told us later that they
had seen him, at one point, standing by the little
basket in the nursery, shaking with sobs.

over and over, i reminded them both they could
change their minds. though clark and ann had come a
long way, they wanted—just as will and i wanted—
for this to be right. they loved devin and dawn.

i didn't get home in time to witness the moments of
clark and ann's time with devin and dawn in the
hospital. i know there were many tears shed by all
. . . prayers . . . sadness and joy. clark and ann
brought the baby home friday evening, and i returned
saturday afternoon. will and clark had left early that
morning with devin, taking him on a fishing trip.
i hurried in, so excited and eager to see charissa, the
new baby. we had emptied all the stuffed animals out
of the bassinet in the nursery and fixed it up for her.
ann had brought her home in the same little white-

and
with
the
gift
came
laugh
·ter·
♥

smocked lace-trimmed gown that i had used with
taylor and brock. it was a sentimental moment . . . we
wanted to tell our children, as they grow up together,
of the camaraderie and fun of this magical experience.

ann was so sweet. "ann, i am so glad you are home.
i cannot remember how to do things . . . it seems so
long since seanne was this age. can you help me?"

i gave charissa her first bath . . . brushed her hair in a
little curl on top . . . fed and burped her. that night
after her feeding, she slept the entire night . . . two
days old! we celebrated.

as it came time to sign the final parental release
papers, dawn went through a wrenching struggle.
i spent hours on the phone with her, letting her cry,
listening to her. it was so important for it to be her
decision . . . one she could live with all her life. finally
i said, "dawn, i just think we ought to dress charissa,
and you and devin come and get her. clark and ann
will love you just the same. i do not want you to do
something you will never feel peace about. let's talk
about how you can manage it if you keep her."

we discussed the realities. the rent. devin's job. the
budget. i loved this couple dearly, and i loved clark
and ann as if they were part of my blood family. it was
an exhausting, emotional time. i understood both
sides and felt that i was in the middle. i longed for
God's wisdom to guide all of us into a truth that
would bring peace and contentment for all concerned.

i believe that if the decision is really right for the birth
mother, it is also right for the prospective adoptive
couple. if a girl decides to keep her baby, God will
have a better plan . . . a more perfect program . . . for
the couple who are longing to adopt a baby.

and
with
the
gift
came
laugh
·ter·

after my last conversation with dawn about coming to get the baby, we hung up and i prepared clark, ann, and seanne. "but i want charissa to be my baby," seanne sobbed.

"if she is the right baby for us, seanne, we will get to keep her," said clark quietly.

moments later the phone rang. "ann, it's dawn. we both just know the baby should be with clark and ann. it's the most wonderful thing that can happen to her. we do not want to change anything."

there was peace and true resolve in her voice. the next day dawn and devin went to the magistrate and signed the papers. later that same day, our phone rang. clark's father, who had planned to pick them up when they flew to boise . . . eagerly anticipating his new granddaughter . . . had died of a heart attack.

fresh, brand-new life had come into their family. another, older life had been taken. joy and sorrow. gain and loss. yes, Jesus gives, and Jesus takes . . . and whatever He does, i have come to trust and believe, is good.

clark, ann, seanne, and charissa are doing famously back in germany, where clark is working on his doctorate. dawn and her mother recently had lunch with me. dawn is as sweet and pretty as ever, and she says she feels absolutely at peace with her decision. she and devin still date, but the relationship has cooled somewhat. we hope that when charissa and rebecca are eighteen years old, each of them will want to meet her birth mother.

our household was back to normal . . . it seemed actually quiet with only two babies . . . nothing stirring but pancakes for breakfast and stories to read

and our little family playing games together again.
but we are bonded to all these people in a unique
way, and not for anything would we have wanted to
miss being a part of their celebration . . . ribbons and
balloons . . . stars on the windows . . . and little
babies safe in loving homes, growing strong and
self-reliant, and creative. helping to change the world.

♥♥
♥♥

of course, not all attempts at adoption go smoothly.

i would be unfair if i gave that impression. recently i had a very difficult, painful experience concerning adoption. i received a call from a girl here in idaho. she had been a fan of my books since she was young. now, in her early twenties, she was eight and a half months pregnant . . . and needing help.

"ann, i feel there is only one thing i can do, and that is to give the baby up. i am going to school and working only part-time. do you think you could find me a really good family? i would like you to pick them."

just that day i had received letters from two couples . . . one in the southeast and the other here in the state, only a few hours away from

and
with
the
gift
came
laugh
·ter·

our home. i suggested to the girl (we'll call her beth) that i drive to her home and see her and her parents. we could talk about all the options . . . make sure she really wanted to do this. i assured her that i would bring a couple of families' resumés, and she could choose one. i knew both of the couples who wanted to adopt . . . tremendous people. i leaned toward the one in idaho, however, because the delivery was to be so soon, and adopting within the state is so much simpler. idaho is an especially ideal state for adoptions.

the next morning i packed my babies into their car seats and started the long drive to beth's home to meet with her and her mother. although i had known and loved beth as long as i had been in idaho, i had never met her parents. her father is a professional man. i looked forward to meeting her mother. i wondered what beth would look like so late in her pregnancy. i was still somewhat in shock from learning about her situation.

her parents' home was charming. i had always admired beth's creativity . . . she had certainly inherited her mother's flair. her mother spoke first. she and beth's father had known about the pregnancy for only a week. because of beth's bone structure, it had been easy for her to conceal her condition by wearing bigger and bigger sweaters. for a long time they just thought beth was gaining a lot of weight. beth announced that she had been to the doctor the day before and was already dilated four centimeters.

i began by letting her and her mother express all their feelings. beth had a history of conflicts with her father, and this had created a lot of stress in her parents' marriage. her mother, very attractive and

and
with
the
gift
came
laugh
·ter·

♥

warm, felt her marriage would be even more strained
if beth kept the baby. they were hurt that their daughter had waited nearly to term to tell them—and then
only because they had suspected and had pressed her
for the truth. they felt they could not bail her out
. . . that she needed to make it on her own. beth
seemed to agree that she was not ready for a baby . . .
neither financially or in other ways. yes, definitely,
she would release the baby, and she felt very positive
about the idaho couple.

i had left taylor and brock with a friend . . . a wonderful mother who cared for my two and her own three
children. it was getting late. i prayed with beth and
her mother and said good-bye, knowing i had a long
drive home. it was an emotional time for me as well
as for them. i had just been through the two adoptions of carrie's and dawn's babies . . . had had house
guests for weeks . . . had traveled with the babies to
my speaking engagements. now beth was due any
moment, and there was a lot of work to do before
that delivery. just when i longed for a breather!

a girl's mother plays such an important role in the
girl's decision. that is why i felt so strongly about
meeting beth's mother and getting her input. with
both taylor and brock, we had talked to their mothers'
families, getting acquainted on the phone. we felt it
was important for our boys to have the blessing not
only of their birth mothers but of their biological
grandparents. we really believed it was important to
their security to have unity and peace within the
entire family.

i called sandi and brent, the prospective parents. i
reminded them that there could not be an absolute
guarantee that the mother would release the baby.

and
with
the
gift
came
laugh
·ter·

♥

there never is, but it was especially true in this situation, where i had not had time to spend with the birth mother. a girl really needs to work all the options through in her mind several weeks before delivery to have faced and confirmed her feelings . . . her decision. when that is accomplished before delivery, it is unusual for the girl to change or vacillate about the decision later, whether the decision is to keep or release the baby.

brent and sandi are a lovely couple. he has an excellent job in a large corporation. she stays home full-time with their three-year-old, lindsey. they had adopted her through an agency and correspond regularly with the birth mother . . . through the agency . . . although they have never met her. lindsey is beautiful . . . looks a lot like sandi. also, sandi is very creative and lindsey's birth mother is too . . . this little baby would fit right in. i felt wonderful about this couple as parents for beth's baby. so excited and elated.

beth called early one morning, a few days later, to say she was going to the hospital. i had promised her i would come and be her labor coach. her mother would be there, too, but was nervous, since it had been more than twenty years since she had had a baby. i was reluctant to leave my babies, because i love being at home with them . . . being in on every bit of their development. sometimes i don't leave the house for two or three days at a time, except to take the boys for a walk. nevertheless, i felt i had a mission to help beth, so i dropped the babies off with my dear friend denise, who has three little girls who love my boys. taylor and brock were as happy as can be to stay there. it would be twelve hours before i headed home that night. it was friday, my usual day at the office. the mail would just have to wait!

and
with
the
gift
came
laugh
·ter·

beth's labor went very quickly. her obstetrician was a woman i had never met. beth was fond of her, and she seemed really to care about beth. her manner toward me, however, was very cold and abrupt . . . almost hostile. at one point i followed her out of the labor room to talk to her.

"i am ann anderson. beth has asked me to find adoptive parents for her baby. i have assured her that she can change her mind when the baby comes, if she wishes. i sense that you are angry about something, and you seem to be directing your anger to me or to beth's mother. let's talk about it."

"well," the doctor snapped, "i just feel her parents are forcing her to give up this baby, and i resent it." she continued to be cold. distant.

"look," i replied, "i have met her family. they are solid, fine people. there is so much you do not know about the situation. beth came to you very late in her pregnancy. she didn't tell her family until a week ago. i assure you that they are not forcing her to do any-thing. they *are* very concerned that the baby be taken care of, and they don't feel it should be their responsi-bility. they want beth to be accountable."

she nodded. i walked out. it occurred to me that this doctor was reacting very personally to beth's situation. i wondered why. one thing was for sure. i did not want her clouding the picture with hostility. first, it was not professional. also, the situation was already painful and traumatic enough for everyone.

one of beth's younger sisters came and stayed with us. she was terrific. she pushed and rubbed beth during contractions. i held beth's hand . . . did the breathing with her . . . fed her ice chips. at 2 p.m. she was

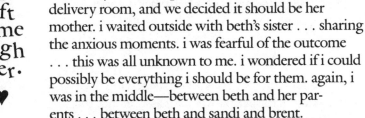

suddenly prepared for the delivery room. they would allow only one extra person to be with her in the delivery room, and we decided it should be her mother. i waited outside with beth's sister . . . sharing the anxious moments. i was fearful of the outcome . . . this was all unknown to me. i wondered if i could possibly be everything i should be for them. again, i was in the middle—between beth and her parents . . . between beth and sandi and brent.

it was almost a full hour before we heard a peep out of the delivery room. instantly the door swung open and the nurse rushed by with a pink bundle. a girl! she had delivered a little girl. her sister burst into tears, and we ran to the window as they laid a beautiful, black-haired baby on the scales. over eight pounds. beth's father appeared with a bouquet of fresh flowers in his hand. a winsome man . . . i liked him instantly.

then began the vigil of pain and tears and strong emotions. beth immediately began to feel she could not release the baby. she loved her too much. she had not known she would feel this way. those feelings are very common with birth mothers, regardless of their decision. the difference was that beth had not given herself and her family enough time to work things through adequately.

beth had no crib. no baby clothes. a part-time job. i hated the thought of the baby's being dropped off every morning at a sitter's and coming home late every evening. there was no father (the birth father had deserted beth the minute he heard she was pregnant). i knew sandi and brent so well. they represented security and stability. the baby mattered so much to me. still, i wanted to be unbiased. my role

and
with
the
gift
came
laugh
·ter·

was not to make beth's decision for her . . . only to guide her . . . to help her come to peace . . . to help her family. however, i was still a novice at this. it was a learning experience.

about 7 p.m. i ate some dinner beth's family brought in. i talked to her parents . . . agreeing with them that it seemed best for beth to give up the baby. yet, we knew there was tremendous emotion in her. there had been a lot of denial, even in beth's not telling her doctor that she was not married.

it was time for me to leave. i said to beth, "i will call tomorrow morning. if you want brent and sandi to have the baby, you can tell me then." i hugged her and her family and stumbled out, feeling more spent than when i had run 26.2 miles. will had picked up our babies, played with them, put them to bed. they were asleep in their cribs when i finally arrived at home.

the next morning i called, trying not to show any emotion or pressure in my voice. "beth, what do you feel?"

"tell them to come and get the baby."

"you are sure?"

"yes."

will and i had made plans to take the babies to jackson hole for a day's outing with their grandmother and a visiting friend. it was hard to leave, but my family comes first, and we had all counted on this day of fun and adventure. i called brent and sandi to tell them the news. they would drive to idaho falls that night and i would meet them the next morning, to drive to the hospital. all the legal details had been worked out

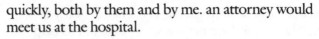

and
with
the
gift
came
laugh
·ter·

quickly, both by them and by me. an attorney would
meet us at the hospital.

i was glad for the opportunity to get away on this
little trip. the closer i got to jackson, the happier i felt.
this was a welcome relief from the intense experience
with beth and her family . . . and i had been totally
absorbed in it.

on sunday i called beth. "do you still feel the same?"
i asked.

"i have not changed my mind since yesterday."

"beth, i will be over in a couple of hours."

will was up early that morning and awakened the
babies . . . changed their diapers . . . fixed their
breakfast while i dressed. will went ahead of us to
church, and the babies and i picked sandi and brent
up. we stopped by the church, where i left one child
in the nursery and the other in a little class. it was
important to me for will to meet this couple. i trust
his judgment, his wisdom. we met briefly, and i could
tell will liked them . . . their gentle strength and
authenticity. and so we set off for beth's town.

the attorney was waiting for us at the hospital. sandi
had brought special little things to dress the baby in.
she and lindsey had prayed every day, for over a year,
that God would give them another baby. lindsey was
with friends back home . . . very, very excited.

leaving brent and sandi with the attorney, i took the
elevator up to beth's room. we would visit a little, and
then i would have the attorney bring her the release
papers to sign. then brent and sandi could take the
baby home. when i walked into beth's room, she was
in the bathroom. the nurse, now familiar to me, came
in and smiled.

and
with
the
gift
came
laugh
·ter·

"i am here because beth is releasing the baby to adoptive parents," i said simply.

"oh, has she changed her mind? she told me earlier this morning that she had decided to keep the baby."

i sat there, frozen. the couple was downstairs . . . the attorney. she had told them to come. what was happening? where were her parents? where did i go from here?

my mind flashed back to the time, several years ago, when will and i had flown to the east coast, diaper bag on my arm, to pick up a baby. it had been agreed that on his thirtieth day we were to come and get him. he was now thirty days old. we had had some painful losses. we anticipated this baby so much. when we arrived at the designated city, the attorney informed us that the mother had changed her mind. i had been where brent and sandi were. will and i had lived through it. it had worked for good in our lives. oh, we cannot even imagine what it would have been to get that baby and not taylor! i knew, whatever happened, brent and sandi could make it.

beth came out of the bathroom. "beth, the nurse was just here and said you told her you were going to keep the baby."

"ann, it is not that easy. i don't feel right about giving her up. i just don't know how i can."

"beth, let's talk about how you would take care of her . . . about the things you would need. is it better for the baby to stay with you? let's work through it."

i loved this girl . . . had cared about beth and prayed for her for years. but there was much i did not know about her history. i had called another friend of hers . . . someone who knew her well . . . and asked

and
with
the
gift
came
laugh
·ter·

what she felt was right. this friend loved her like a daughter. she seemed to feel the baby needed to go to the adoptive couple, yet felt as confused as i. "ann," she said, "i look at my children and realize that life is hard. a child needs everything possible to make it in life. not having a strong father would be extremely hard. i have shared this with beth."

beth and i continued to talk. i feared, more than anything else, that she would make the wrong decision just because it seemed to be the easy decision. i was even more concerned for her than for brent and sandi. i didn't want her to keep a baby who would grow up to resent her . . . to break her heart. that would be on her conscience for the rest of her life. i sat there by her bed, feeling the urgency of her making the right decision. i am sure that i exerted some pressure on her . . . it was only my third day on this job, and i didn't have a large enough frame of reference to go on.

suddenly, she began to cry and scream, "go get the attorney. NOW. i mean it. i want to sign the papers."

"beth, you must not sign the paper in that spirit. to sign with that attitude would be a terrible mistake. i won't let you do it. why don't i take the baby home with me for a few days while you get all the things ready for her. then you can pick her up. my babies would love that."

"ann," she pleaded, "go get that lawyer. i want to do it now."

i left her room in a daze . . . in a way i felt numb . . . but ready to crack. what constituted manipulation? what was truth? what was my place? i realized i was in an powerful position. i could not let beth do

and
with
the
gift
came
laugh
·ter·

something in that distraught state and then point her finger at me the rest of my life, making me assume the blame. this was her life . . . her decision. and i had to protect myself.

when i found her parents in the waiting room, i broke down.

"ann, it is right for her to sign the paper. she must," her father announced with conviction.

i looked at her mother. "yes," she said. "i feel as he does. it just would not be right for the baby not to have what a family can give her. i think this is a decision beth wants us to make for her. then she will not have to do it. i really believe this is what she wants."

again i thought what charming people beth's parents were. i felt they loved her deeply and honestly desired what was right for her. but it was hard.

i went down to the waiting couple and the attorney. sandi's face was wet with tears. she knew there must be a problem. when i told them the situation, they were quiet. though beth had insisted on signing, i had some deep fears about taking a baby under these conditions. i told brent and sandi this. then i suggested we all go to the maternity floor. beth's parents had said they wanted to meet brent and sandi, and the attorney could go with me to beth's room. sandi tucked a little gift into my hand, all wrapped, for beth . . . with a letter . . . and asked me to take them to her.

as the attorney and i walked in, the doctor passed us on her way out. she was very cool. later i was to learn that she had confided to beth that years before, she

and
with
the
gift
came
laugh
·ter·

♥

had given up a baby and always had regretted it terribly.

as the attorney stood there, explaining the legal ramifications, i just prayed. that was all i knew to do. i didn't pray that beth would sign, but that she would do the right thing. at that point, i never would have encouraged her to sign, except that she had demanded to do it. i am sure she felt pressure from everyone. her parents were insisting on it, honestly believing this was best for beth. with her mother standing by her quietly, beth signed. she asked to see the baby one more time, so i sent a nurse to get her.

as the attorney left, beth began to scream at me, "you lied! you lied to me!"

her mother tried to calm her down, and i just stared . . . too confused and hurt to speak. finally i asked softly, "how did i lie, beth? i have strong, deep convictions against lying. nothing could hurt me more than for you to accuse me of that. tell me, why you are saying this?"

"i told you this morning on the phone that i had not changed my mind since yesterday. you talked to my mother last night, and she told you i was going to keep the baby. why did you bring everyone in here?"

"beth, i never spoke to your mother last night. i only saw her a few minutes ago out here in the waiting room. all i knew was that yesterday morning you told me to have brent and sandi come."

beth looked confused. her mother said, "beth, ann and i did not talk at all yesterday."

she now knew i had not lied, but it was too late to heal the situation. there had been too much turmoil . . . too many hurtful words. i was just a friend,

and
with
the
gift
came
laugh
·ter·

caught in the middle, spending a lot of time and energy for nothing . . . no kindness or gratitude. she was just a young woman, forced to make the biggest decision of her life at her weakest moment.

brent and sandi took the baby. beth's father had asked us to wait to leave the hospital until he had a chance to get beth to the car. the nursery nurse walked out with the baby, and as that is hospital policy, she stated she would have to carry the baby to the exit door.

"please," i begged. "we don't want to leave yet. can't we just wait in this corner until the birth mother has left? we feel it is important not to run into her."

"oh, i know a shortcut. another way out. we will take it," she announced, marching quickly ahead of us.

"nurse," i pleaded again, "a shortcut is not the issue. please let us wait."

we were all worried, but she was far ahead of us. finally we gave up and followed, feeling helpless. as we walked out the door, the nurse ahead of us, we nearly walked into the car carrying beth and her parents as they were leaving. another nightmare. a heartbreaking moment. as brent and sandi got into their car, sandi was crying. "i feel as if we are stealing her baby," she sobbed.

we all felt physically ill. that last moment, of looking up and seeing beth in the car, was the final blow. i rode with brent and sandi and the darling new baby back to idaho falls. they stopped at our home long enough to change the baby and show her to brock and taylor. i hugged them, and then they headed home, enraptured with their tiny bundle. i was a basket case the rest of the evening. will's strength and the babies' laughter and games comforted my bruised, wounded emotions.

and
with
the
gift
came
laugh
·ter·

♥

"ann," will commented, "if we had been the ones picking up that baby, we would have walked out, refusing to take her. we will never take a baby whose birth mother cannot give her total blessing and release the child in the right spirit. there are no easy answers for beth . . . but one thing is for sure—brent and sandi are pure quality!"

the next week was thanksgiving. each year we spend that day with will's mother and some close friends, lee and nancy. it is always such a happy time. i was so eagerly looking forward to it, and i tried not to think about beth and that whole ordeal. one thing i realized more clearly than ever before . . . placing babies can be one of the most exhausting, draining experiences in the world. if i was going to continue to do this, i must count the cost and decide if it was worth it, to myself, my husband, my two little sons.

on the day before thanksgiving i received a call from brent and sandi. beth had called them, saying she had not gone through with signing the final papers at the courthouse. she wanted to pick up the baby the next day . . . thanksgiving day. meanwhile, brent's parents had flown in from colorado to celebrate the new baby. a shower had been given. lindsey adored her baby sister. now the baby was going back to beth.

will and i drove to see beth's parents that night. it was hard, but we felt we had to go, we cared so deeply about them. will wanted to meet them face to face. we requested that beth not be there. she had made her decision . . . now it was time to minister to her parents.

they were so gracious. we talked and shared over popcorn and soft drinks. again i felt keenly that they were stable people who deeply loved beth and the

and
with
the
gift
came
laugh
·ter·

baby. they were worried . . . frantic. we reminded
beth's dad that anger would only destroy him. we
prayed together . . . that God would be redemptive
in all our lives through this learning experience.

that night beth's mother went to see beth one more
time at her apartment. she reminded her of all the
issues that seemed important concerning the baby.
beth wanted her sister to go with her in her little car
to pick up the baby, but the family decided that if this
was beth's decision, she should carry it out alone.

i called brent and sandi. they were dissolved in tears
and grief. "ann," sandi wept, "we love this baby so
much. we feel as if she is our own baby. we don't
know how we are going to live through this."

"sandi, i am so sorry. i feel terribly sad. you and brent
will make it. you are strong, solid people. that is why
i chose you. if this is not your baby, then God has
closed the door . . . but he will open another door for
you sometime. i beg you and brent not to be angry
when beth comes. i will be praying."

sandi called back an hour later. "ann, the baby's gone.
when we opened the door to beth, we suddenly felt
so much love for her. we didn't hate her or feel angry.
we wrapped our arms around her and cried with her.
i dressed the baby in a new little outfit i had bought,
with a new receiving blanket, and a little teddy bear.
we prayed with beth and then brent carried the baby
to the car. we told her that if she changed her mind,
she could call us. God really was with us, ann. it was
sort of like abraham giving up isaac, but we are doing
okay."

brent and sandi and lindsey are still waiting for a
baby. beth has her little girl. she has found a good

and
with
the
gift
came
laugh
·ter·

baby-sitter, and still goes to school and works part-time. she says she is very happy . . . that it was the right decision. that her mother feels relieved now and has come to believe she did the best thing. that her father adores the baby.

i still care deeply for beth. the crisis is over for now, at least. the wounds are still healing, and we have battle scars. this experience taught me many things: to remain absolutely neutral . . . not to open myself to too much emotional entanglement . . . to try to know a girl really well before i involve myself with her. and not to be afraid to call brent and sandi again someday, with another potential adoption. i must not walk away forever from exposing myself to birth mothers and the opportunity to help them and love them. i pray i can watch as other couples are blessed with children.

more than ever i respect the great courage girls exhibit when they make a decision concerning their babies. i must not forget that my task is not to decide the fate of the baby . . . only to be a tool, an instrument of God's peace and love.

CHAPTER 9

letters i receive from the readers of my books

often bring me just the word of encouragement or of challenge i need. some of the letters i've received about being a mother are especially challenging . . . like the one from a woman who said that she feels so much more beautiful inside, knowing that i have all the same emotions she has.

she said, "i like myself so much better after your sharing." she has three little children and just can't handle all three of them by herself out in public. "i can't even go out for a hamburger without one of them spilling a coke and catsup on my white slacks . . . and another of them having a horrible diaper during lunch!" she adds, "after one such experience, i came home, put the kids down for a nap, and

and
with
the
gift
came
laugh
·ter·

opened your book. after i read it, i was a new person! wish you could come and have lunch with me some-time. . . ."

another girl wrote, "ann, i want to share with you something i foresee that you will have to deal with soon. i had two tubal pregnancies when i was young . . . lost both babies and both tubes, so, like you, i have struggled with feeling incomplete and inadequate. i also have two adopted children . . . both are hyperactive, but wonderful, beautiful, precious gifts.

"God gave me these kids who have especially big needs . . . and i feel responsible to do a better job for them than their birth mothers could have done. . . . in fact, since God was so gracious to answer my prayers to be a mother, i *must not fail* . . . i have to be Super Mom. but i *do* fail. there doesn't seem to have been much written about adoption and trying to be a Super Mom, but i think it is a big issue, and it all centers on the issue of self-esteem and worthiness, which you speak to so effectively. i keep thinking that if these were my biological children, i would have known instinctively what to do for them . . . but these kids are a mystery to me, and i so frequently fail them."

i felt these letters should be shared. one woman has three natural children; the other has two adopted children. both struggle. both have discovered that motherhood is a complex, all-consuming adventure. my sister jan . . . mother, therapist, writer . . . says every child, adopted or natural, has difficult issues to deal with. and that every mother has fears and in-adequacies and struggles with the unknown.

and
with
the
gift
came
laugh
·ter·

i do have these fears and struggles. often it is just impossible for me to evaluate the quality of my mothering. unless you have been there, you cannot understand what two babies under the age of two can do—and undo—in five minutes. and every five minutes thereafter! they do not mean to be bad. they are just simply making ingenious attempts to enter- tain themselves. the largest audience i have ever addressed seems easy and uncomplicated compared to playing with . . . cleaning up after . . . disciplining my two toddlers.

example: yesterday the sun was warm and inviting. the boys were dressed in fresh shirts and oshkosh overalls, with white socks and sweaters. i told them they could play in our backyard. a few minutes later i heard them both screaming. when i went to investi- gate, there they were . . . both in the neighbor's yard, where a pond is being built. they were stuck in the mud and could not get out. the white socks were invisible, because there was mud up to their ankles. balancing on a board, i pulled and pulled, one child at a time. they finally popped out . . . sneakers still submerged in mud . . . with me fighting to keep my balance. it had taken thirty minutes to get them dressed, combed, noses wiped, coats and hats on. five minutes for them to be covered in mud . . . and nothing to do but completely strip them and start over!

although i keep trying to resolve my fears, i continu- ally am afraid that when taylor and brock get older, they will somehow resent me. i've struggled so much with the brutal pain of my inability to produce a child . . . such a potent sense of defectiveness. will the babies feel i am defective, too? will they resent having

and
with
the
gift
came
laugh
·ter·

♥

me for a mother? how can i ever be good enough for these little boys i love more than my own life? today we have an intimate, deep relationship and bond. but when they begin to realize fully what their adoption means, how will they feel? what if my strengths do not compensate for my flaws?

everything i read says that adopted children should be made to understand their adoption as early as possible. when taylor was barely two, i read stories to him about being adopted. i love how our boys came into our lives. i cherish their mothers. i feel such warm pleasure when i see little evidences of them in their babies. it is all very special to me and to will. i just want taylor and brock to be happy about it too. it's interesting to me that will does not have the same uncertainties i have . . . he is very secure about these things.

jan says that when she scrubs her kitchen floor, she knows whether it is clean or dirty . . . but with children, there are never black-and-white answers . . . no guarantees. she has a clever, brilliant friend who says she would have gone through life feeling like a wonderful person if she had never had children and had to be a successful mother! smile.

sometimes people say things like . . . "that girl is a real problem child . . . but of course, she's adopted." or "their son is such a rebel. it's heartbreaking . . . must be linked to his being adopted." "well, what can you expect from that child . . . rejected by her own mother?" many of us, especially those who have had no experience or real knowledge about adoption, feel that all adopted children are rebellious misfits. we may form this bigoted opinion and carry it with us all our lives, spreading it to all those we talk to.

and
with
the
gift
came
laugh
·ter·

this makes me understand better why some adoptive parents tend to smother and overprotect and over-indulge their children. it is something will and i are working very hard not to do, but i can certainly understand the temptation. our comprehension of the process is so limited, and our fears of rejection are so great.

as i have mentioned before, i am convinced that most birth mothers never "reject" their children. the birth mother does something more noble than many of us would be capable of—she sacrifices her own natural affection for her child . . . her own ambitions and love for her baby . . . hoping to give the child much, much more than she could give it, especially the gift of a complete family.

one birth mother we know, "laurie," wrote to the adoptive parents of her child:

i was surprised and totally unprepared for how much i would love her and want her. all during my pregnancy i never really wanted to have the responsibility of raising a child . . . but when i saw her, suddenly the whole world changed, and i wanted her . . . i wanted to keep her and hold her and love her and teach her and experience her in every way, forever and ever. i know you can understand my devotion and attachment as you grow to love her more deeply each day.

but now, because of God's abundant grace in you, i no longer wonder if i did the right thing. i know i did, and i thank you for being there for her. i hope you can understand that i can't help but always love her, and i will never cease to pray for and miss her as well. . . . i never knew that i could be so changed and so much better and stronger and more beautiful because of such a

and
with
the
gift
came
laugh
·ter·

♥

happening. and i never knew i could draw so near to the Lord and receive such comfort and hope and understanding.

Thank you for having room in your heart to spare and to share. i can't tell you of the great peace it gave me to know of your love for Christ, of your devotion to family and friends, of your intentions to instruct her in God's Word and to introduce her to Jesus—and of all your provisions for her that i could not give, especially of your love for her—to be there with her to play, and talk, and feed, and clean, and teach, and mostly to snuggle and cuddle and hold and comfort her. that is what i most want for her from you.

one Christmas will and i took the babies to the dominican republic. our dear friends herb and dona and their two grown daughters were with us, along with a charming older couple, the olfords. taylor and brock were the only children in the group. we all stayed in a spacious house, with large bedrooms and private baths. a full-time maid, romalita, did our laundry and cared for the children, playing with them and getting them ready for bed most evenings.

we adults had many vibrant, stimulating conversations over delightful dinners. we would tuck the boys into bed . . . sing carols . . . pray together. we had many talks about our inner struggles. one night dona looked at me and said, "ann, you talk so much about how smart taylor is. i wonder if you really hear yourself?"

here was someone i love and trust, telling me something that frightened me. something i needed to hear. i knew she loved me, and i knew that there is at least an element of truth in almost all criticism or correction. while the other adults continued to chat, i went quietly to our room. the babies were sleeping. i lay

down next to brock and gazed at him. he is so beautiful . . . olive skin . . . huge, liquid brown eyes . . . natural curls . . . such an easy, sweet disposition. i kissed
his limp little fingers and his rosy cheek. he never
stirred. he and taylor look so much like brothers that
no one even questions it. often in a store, a sales clerk
will smile at me and comment, "my! there's no doubt
that those two are brothers!" and, of course, will and
i could never love one of them more than the other.

next, i crept over to taylor's bed. watching him sleep
has always been one of my favorite pastimes. he looks
especially like liz when he is asleep. i have always been
fascinated at how his mind grasps things so quickly
. . . how he never forgets words and details . . . used
good grammar from the beginning and seemed
instinctively to know verb tenses. when he was my
only baby and i had more time, i would sit by his crib
and wonder what actually went on in his head. i will
never forget one morning when i went back to sleep
after will left. taylor woke up and climbed out of his
crib and walked into our room. he stood by me,
kissing my face, not making a sound . . . and smiling
when i opened my eyes.

lying there beside him that night, i began to try to
work through my feelings about him. why would i
brag so much about taylor's intelligence? did other
people feel that i did this, too? was i afraid brock, now
the baby, was going to outshine him? did i feel that
taylor had not had enough time to be the baby of the
family and receive all the attention? was i perhaps
worried that people would not value him as much
because he was adopted . . . so i had to keep remind-
ing them how special taylor really was? was this a
result of my having grown up in a family . . . in a
society . . . where brains and education were so
significant in assessing one's value? brock was still too

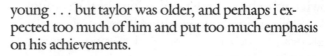

and
with
the
gift
came
laugh
·ter·

♥

young . . . but taylor was older, and perhaps i ex-
pected too much of him and put too much emphasis
on his achievements.

oh, how i loved him! he was my soul child . . . my
first miracle baby. he traveled everywhere with me,
relieving some of the great loneliness i felt on the
road. we ate together . . . learned songs . . . read
books . . . played together under the dining table.
(now he and brock play there together.) taylor was so
young when brock came that he might have felt
displaced. i wanted—and still want—each baby to
feel equally loved . . . equally valuable. where had i
read that studies prove that it is harder on children to
be overprotected than to experience the pains and
injustices of life?

i began to pray . . . "Jesus, show me what it is that i
fear for taylor, so i will not flaunt him or push him or
overprotect him. so that i will be relaxed and allow
him to be himself." i realized that it was easier for me
to do that with the second baby. when brock came, i
was much more relaxed and secure about parenting.
as i prayed, some understanding came to me. taylor is
a lot like me—extremely sensitive. he will hurt more
in life . . . be more intuitive. i want him to feel secure,
but i must not try so hard to protect him from hurts.

one day in the doctor's office, the nurse came in and
chatted with the boys. as she was leaving, she looked
at brock and said, "isn't he a darling!" taylor listened
and watched. taylor is blond and blue-eyed and
darling too, but he is no longer the baby. people
often make remarks like that about my baby, while
taylor stands by and listens. he is the older one . . .
considered a "big boy" although less than a year older
than brock. this experience has made me more sensitive to the feelings of other children who have ador-

and
with
the
gift
came
laugh
·ter·

able baby siblings. jan says it was very painful for her, when her second son was born and tre was only three . . . and simply could not compete with that darling new baby. adults can be so insensitive about this. i realize that i must build into my babies' consciousness that they are whole and strong and special, regardless of what others say or do.

now that we are watching brock grow, we see that he is quickly developing words and sentences. we are delighted at how bright he is too. it pleases us that the boys are becoming such good friends.

sometimes people suggest that it is too bad that we have not had children of our own. we have not totally given up hope of my carrying a pregnancy to term, but we honestly believe we could not have produced brighter, more healthy, strong, beautiful children than taylor and brock. (sometimes we even laugh about it and say we wonder what kind of kids we would have produced!)

so, watching taylor sleep that night, i realized that it is tiresome for others to have to listen too much to a prejudiced mother or grandmother. to hear how fabulous and perfect and special their babies are. really secure people talk less about themselves and their children, and more about you and your interests. they are more honest about their struggles and the frailty of their humanity, rather than working so hard to impress others with glory and great success.

that night in the dominican marked a significant step in my life as a mother. i have been learning not to brag about taylor's traits. oh, i forget sometimes—in insecure moments—but i am a lot farther down the road. taylor is strong enough to hold his own, to find his own place. we are watching him do it so well. he is

**and
with
the
gift
came
laugh
·ter·**

♥

a hero to his little brother, who wants to do *everything* just the way taylor does it. and he's a shining star to us!

motherhood is a magnificent but frightening experience. the reality is that we are all imperfect . . . all so human . . . all flawed. both natural and adoptive parents make mistakes. every day i beg for grace and wisdom from God. i pray every time i reach for "the spoon," wanting never to discipline my children in anger or frustration. in the end, it is not how perfect and ingenious a mother i am . . . it matters only that i learn to hear my boys . . . that i let them talk to me about their feelings (positive or negative) concerning friends, school, or adoption. that i really listen. that i be an authentic person . . . real. willing to grow and be flexible.

if taylor and brock can see that we love and accept them, unconditionally, and are consistent in our own lives, then i feel they can make it all the way. as an imperfect mother, i plead every day, "make me more like you, Father. create in me a clean heart."

dr. bruce narramore
tells parents that
human beings have
at least three
basic emotional needs.

often i have sat and listened to my
sister jan discuss these needs, and i
have come to understand them
and desire their fulfillment for my
own children. every day, in small
ways, i try to touch my little sons
in these three areas.

the first is their need to feel loved.
jan tells me that we can encourage
our children to feel loved by eye
contact, physical touch, and
focused attention.

"taylor, look at mommy . . . look
in my eyes. i love you!" and he
laughs.

"brock, look at mommy. brock!
look in my eyes. i think you are
fantastic!" i kiss his soft, plump
cheek and squeeze him.

and
with
the
gift
came
laugh
·ter·

♥

we do lots of touching at our house. every evening will and i get down on the floor with taylor and brock. (and i often do this during the day, too.) they crawl up on will's back and he takes them for rides around the room. we tackle daddy. we tickle. we throw the babies on the bed.

tom and jan, and will and i, all do a little game with our boys. we take one of their hands and squeeze it three times for "i love you." they squeeze back twice for "how much?" then we grip their small hands as tightly as they can stand it, to mean, "sooo much!" nothing could be more precious to me the rest of my life than feeling my babies' little hands squeezed in mine. often when they crawl up next to me on the couch or in bed, brock or taylor will say, "hold my hand, mommy." dear, tender moments!

when it comes to focused attention, i do not know of anyone who knows how to do that better than my sister. she takes her little boys, separately, on walks. to k-mart with fifty cents and shops with them for an hour. eats ice-cream cones and listens to them tell her their most intimate feelings. one must teach children to do that . . . vulnerability is not a natural response with most of us.

one of my favorite memories is of something that happened last spring. will would come home every day at noon and pick up the babies in their dress coats and hats and tights to keep their legs warm. they would all go to one of will's favorite fishing holes. two fishing poles, lots of worms, and absolute glee. hiking through dirt and over rocks, will—in his white shirt and tie and sport coat—and taylor and brock—just toddlers—would fish. the sky so blue and clear. spring sunshine baking the damp earth

and
with
the
gift
came
laugh
•ter•

after its long bout with winter. two little boys and their big strong daddy.

i went along once to watch. will and taylor, both holding the same pole, were pulling in the line with a big fish on it. before i knew what was happening, the hook—and the fish—got caught on my sweater. i screamed as the cold, slimy fish flopped against my arm. will tried earnestly to pull the hook out of my sweater. taylor and brock stood by, eyes big, and patted my legs to comfort me.

for the all-time championship in giving focused attention, you can't improve on a grandmother. my mother tells wonderful stories and bakes delicious cookies and knows just how to make the babies feel secure and happy. grandma jo, will's mother, does amazing things for taylor and brock . . . takes them to the library . . . the bank . . . they pick flowers . . . watch gerbils. she fixes picnic lunches on her bedroom floor, with a little teapot and cups. most of the boys' special toys come from grandma jo, and many of their favorite books.

she is always thinking of new, creative things to do for them. she gets out her tape recorder and lets them talk and sing into it, and then lets them listen to their voices. when taylor first learned to use the potty, she bought him a tow truck. brock got a dump truck. taylor and brock adore her.

with two babies just eleven months apart, i have found privacy almost nil. when i go to the bathroom, they are there. when i take a bath, they beg to get in too, and i usually succumb because they love it so much. nowadays, when i pull out a box of cheerios or raisin bran or froot loops to eat, i can pretty well assume they have been all over the floor, then

and
with
the
gift
came
laugh
·ter·

gathered in sweaty little hands and put back into the boxes. they *love* dumping boxes of cereal on the floor!

jan says that the substitute need for feeling loved is the need for attention. when children constantly demand everyone's attention, it very likely means they need to feel more loved.

one sunday will was to speak in the morning worship service at our church. he forewarned me of what he had in mind, so i had taylor dressed beautifully . . . starched outfit . . . new white tights . . . baby shoes polished . . . hair brushed with a curl on top . . . scrubbed and then covered with sweet baby lotion.

at a certain point in his presentation, will asked taylor if he would come up to the platform. taylor was just a year old. i stood him on the floor and he toddled toward will. the closer he got to his daddy, the faster he walked. by the time will reached out to scoop him up in his arms, taylor was nearly running on his chunky baby legs. it was a magic, spontaneous moment . . . full of love. taylor was completely oblivious to the congregation and totally absorbed with his father. will had brought one of taylor's favorite little books, and together they talked and laughed and shared its story, while the spellbound audience observed.

will's message was on the power of prayer . . . that if you go through life without praying and believing, you will be cheated of some beautiful miracles. taylor was our answer to prayer . . . our miracle. will gave taylor his focused attention. everyone celebrated.

the second emotional need a child has is to feel confident. he tends to develop this through what he

and
with
the
gift
came
laugh
·ter·

experiences. jan tells a story about nash, her eight-year-old, who had three goals he wanted to achieve one summer: to tie his shoes, to learn how to pump a swing, and to ride his bicycle without training wheels. as he accomplished each one of those goals, his confidence soared.

when taylor was eleven months old and brock a newborn, i would ask taylor if he could bring me a diaper for brock. with much pride he would disappear, then return, always with more than one diaper! i would clap and cheer. now brock does the cheering himself.

in the evenings, will teaches the boys how to catch a football and "hike" it . . . how to toss and hit a tennis ball . . . how to ride the tricycles that grandma gave them. their faces glow with pride and strength as they develop new skills.

the child's confidence is also displayed when he learns to be assertive . . . to stand up for himself. jan tells a cute story about tre, now ten years old. he was at soccer practice one day when another kid said, "are you a boy or a girl? i can't tell by your hair."

tre casually responded, "i was just getting ready to ask you the same question." he was not going to be intimidated. he left the other little boy speechless.

children need to make "i" statements, as do adults. i am struggling. i am scared. i do not know if you love me. will says that he spent his whole life, before he knew me, never considering his feelings. he just experienced dogged determination to "get the job done." now i often ask him, "honey, what are you feeling?" i do the same thing with taylor and brock . . . on airplanes, before they go to sleep at

and
with
the
gift
came
laugh
·ter·

night, whenever one cries more than usual . . . i always hold them on my lap and we talk.

"mommy, brock frustrates me." "i don't like taylor . . . he hit me."

most of the time i let taylor and brock resolve their own conflicts. i don't often interfere. i do listen to their feelings. i am always challenging them to express them. if i see an injustice, i will discipline.

the need for confidence has its substitute too; it is power and control. dominating adults are generally people who learned as children that only through controlling others could they feel confident.

and the third big need is to feel worthwhile. this is an intrinsic value each child has. it is within a parent's power to help a child feel worthwhile and valuable even if he or she fails or makes a mistake. the child must still feel he or she is liked . . . not only loved, but *liked.*

again, i have received much insight from my sister, and it has helped me as a mother. she says, first of all, to *listen* to what the child is saying. she tells of a private talk she had with tre.

"mommy, sometimes i think you can see everything i do and hear everything i say."

"maybe you feel crowded," jan responded quietly.

"mommy, when mary came over and changed lisa's diaper at our house, i took it out of the trashcan and put it back in her diaper bag," tre confessed.

without reacting, jan commented, "maybe you didn't want it to smell up the house."

and
with
the
gift
came
laugh
·ter·

"mommy, sometimes i have bad feelings about you.
i do not have bad feelings about daddy."

"oh, honey," jan said, "i do have such a hard time
sometimes. and you do have such a wonderful daddy.
i understand why you might feel that way."

taylor and brock are at the stage of screaming "mine"
with their toys. when there is that kind of conflict, i
always try to say, "i know this toy is yours. yes, it
belongs to you. but may sheena play with it? these are
your toys, but you must share."

taylor especially loves books. there is a little rhyme he
knows by heart . . . one that i frequently remind him
of:

selfish sue, selfish sue, with toys of every kind.
you never share! you never share! you say, "mine! mine!"
selfish sue with face so blue, the Bible says, "be kind."
share your toys with girls and boys, and then your face
*   will shine.*

not only is it important to listen to our children in
order for them to feel worthwhile, but we need to
affirm them:

"i am so glad you are learning to think for yourself."

"i am so proud of you for cleaning your room."

"you amazed me when you did that puzzle."

"brock, you are a smart boy. you are learning to say so
many big words. you must be proud of yourself."

while we drive along in the car, taylor will coax brock.
he will call out a word and ask brock to repeat it.
when brock says the word correctly, taylor claps and
cheers, just as we did with him when he was younger.

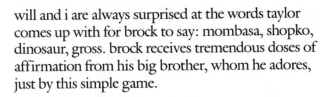

and
with
the
gift
came
laugh
·ter·

will and i are always surprised at the words taylor comes up with for brock to say: mombasa, shopko, dinosaur, gross. brock receives tremendous doses of affirmation from his big brother, whom he adores, just by this simple game.

the firstborn tends to have the advantage in this area of affirmation, because he has had the undivided attention of the parents. there are no siblings with whom to compete. at least, it seems to be that way with taylor. he is always the first one to learn new tricks, and by the time brock gets there, it is easy for us to be casual with our praise . . . not to make such a big deal about everything he does. maybe that is healthier, anyway, but we try to show as much excitement over brock's development as we do with taylor's.

both jan and i sing a little song to our babies:

i like your eyes . . . i like your nose. . . .
i like your mouth, your fingers, and your toes.
i like your face . . . it's really you. . . .
i like the things you say and do!

finally . . . it is very necessary for a child to know forgiveness if he is to feel worthwhile. when i was about ten, i was drying the dinner dishes as jan washed them. we had had company, and my mother had used her finest china—plates, gravy boat, serving dishes. as i was stacking them neatly along the counter, my mother warned me several times to set them farther back. she saw how easy it would be to knock them off. i did not mean to disobey, but i was not listening or responding. in one instant, as i flung the dish towel around to pick up another dish, i saw the towel and my arm wipe all the dishes off the counter. they crashed into hundreds of pieces all over the kitchen floor.

and
with
the
gift
came
laugh
·ter·

♥

the disaster was so great and my responsibility so
heavy, my heart was sick. sobbing, i got down on my
knees and began to pick up all the precious pieces. i
did not know whether i was going to get spanked,
but that seemed unimportant compared to the guilt
and failure i felt. my mother quickly surveyed the
scene and said, "honey, they are only dishes. dishes
can always be replaced. now stop crying and we will
clean it up together."

never will i forget that gesture of profound love and
forgiveness by my mother. i remember it every time
one of my little boys dreams up a new variety of
mischief. it tempers my anger. it clears my head so
i know how to respond and discipline more wisely.

yes, a sense of worth and value has its substitute
too—it is perfectionism. to make straight a's, to be a
star basketball player, to do all the right things and do
them best. perfectionism says, "if i can be perfect
enough and pretty enough and outstanding enough,
then i will know i am worthwhile to my family and to
the world . . . even to myself."

while i was writing this chapter this morning, taylor
awakened. when i held him and told him i was writing
a book about him and brock, he asked for paper and
pen too. so he is sitting at my side and i am cheering
him on as he says, "mommy, look! i can write my
name. t-a-y-r-o . . . oops, i made a mistake. mommy,
let me go check on brock."

and so it's time for me to prepare myself for another
challenging, stretching day of motherhood . . . to
remind you again that i do not have all the answers,
but i am only sharing what i, too, am learning.
motherhood is, for me, the ultimate, glorious adventure. and it means so much to share my dreams and
struggles with you.

CHAPTER 11

so many times
we are cheated out
of laughter because
we get discouraged.
we carry a dream for a little
while . . . for a short leg of the
journey . . . and when nothing
transpires, we give up. we toss the
dream out and stumble down the
road, defeated and pessimistic
about life. our children watch us,
and they learn from us. they have
very little passion for dreams
because we don't.

no great gift . . . no authentic,
vibrant laughter . . . comes without a price. without a dream that
took courage and determination.
boldness. a stretching of one's safe
boundaries. one of will's and my
greatest, deepest desires for our
children is that they embrace
something bigger than themselves.
that they let God plant a dream in

and
with
the
gift
came
laugh
·ter·

♥

them. we don't want them ever to worship the dream . . . only the Giver of the dream. but we want taylor and brock to embrace Him and to expect miracles along the journey. living is too hard . . . reality sometimes too brutal . . . without the dream. they will be cheated out of so many surprises and joys if they do not look for the serendipities God has for them.

today i am in the middle of my life. my dream for motherhood was born in me when i was a small child. it has taken many years—some lonely years— some long stretches of dry desert and tough climbing. waiting until thirty-five to get married gave me much more life content and maturity to bring into marriage. experiencing terribly painful losses through miscarriages and fallen-through adoptions smoothed many rough edges in will's and my hearts. it connected us to thousands who feel the same pain. it filled us with compassion and sensitivity. the pain forced us to connect to deeper feelings in our lives, and we became truly honest people. we are so much more appreciative of taylor and brock. much wiser in our aspirations for them . . . in our parenting.

raymond, a dear friend of will's and mine, is a great man with a rather profound story. years ago, in his youth, he became the greatest wide receiver of all time in professional football. he played for the baltimore colts and is now in football's hall of fame. during that time he became one of will's two boyhood heroes—the other was pancho, the tennis star.

i met raymond and sally many years later, in boston, when he was an assistant coach—very low on the totem pole of power—for the new england patriots. they became two of my dearest friends before i had even met will. i knew them in raymond's lean years.

and
with
the
gift
came
laugh
·ter·

after retiring from professional football, he had
experienced many, many years when finances were
very limited and prestige almost nil. twenty-plus
years of tough preparation for God's plan down the
road. every job along the way . . . each place of
humiliation . . . each struggle . . . brought him closer.
it would have been so easy to toss in the towel. to lose
faith in God. to have used politics to maneuver out of
his pain. but then he would have missed the blessing
in the sunrise.

one night, while having dinner at their home outside
boston, a tiny spark seemed to burst in me. "raymond,
i have an idea . . . a dream. i just feel that some day
you are going to be head coach of the new england
patriots."

he and sally laughed. they said that was impossible.
beyond imagination. raymond had never aspired to
such a position. his desire was simply to follow God
and take whatever job was assigned to him, giving it
his very best.

when will and i married, raymond took me down the
aisle to will. will's boyhood hero handed over his
bride. it seemed so right, since my father was marry-
ing us. there are fairy tales and make-believe, but
God's surprises even outdo the fantasies. oh, our
children must grow up understanding that!

we moved to idaho. years passed. i stubbornly believed, in spite of the lean years for raymond and sally,
that he would become head coach of the patriots. one
night, very late, our phone rang. "ann, it's raymond. i
wanted you and will to be the first to know. i have
just been appointed head coach of the new england
patriots."

midseason, 1985. a miracle. when *God* gives a dream
. . . when we hang on and believe against all odds . . .

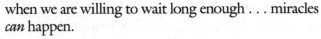

and
with
the
gift
came
laugh
·ter·

♥

when we are willing to wait long enough . . . miracles *can* happen.

as we were falling asleep that night, will said, "well, i am going to take this miracle one step further. i believe God can help raymond take new england to the super bowl his first full year of coaching." it was now midseason. the team had only five or six more games to go before the playoffs. will felt raymond would need a full season to do it.

"honey," i responded, shocked, "that seems impossible! i have watched the team. it has some very gifted players, but they live on the edge of great things, and somehow never seem to cross the line."

"ann, i just believe."

we would race home from church every sunday, flip on the television and wait for the scores to be flashed on the screen. if new england was a goal or touchdown behind, will would get on his knees and pray. if the score got worse, he would call me in and we'd pray together. sometimes he went to the phone, calling friends. "are you watching football? do me a favor, please. pray for the patriots to win."

the team didn't always win. no doubt the other teams had fans who were praying too! but will's spirit of love and caring was there.

will and i were on a flight, with our babies, heading home from the east coast. it was sunday and we hated not being where we could watch the patriots play the final playoff game with miami. will sent a message to the pilot, asking him to announce the scores. "ladies and gentlemen, this is the captain speaking. i've had a request to let you in on the football scores today. the new england patriots will be playing the chicago bears in the super bowl."

and
with
the
gift
came
laugh
·ter·

♥

will and i grabbed taylor and brock and cried and laughed. We squeezed them and kissed them. will let out a piercing "yahoo!" that made the planeful of passengers erupt into laughter. new england on their way to the super bowl. raymond's first full year of coaching. he and God had done it! another dream . . . another miracle painted the sky and danced on the walls.

yes, we were there at the super bowl. free tickets. fantastic seats. memories. so the bears crunched the patriots. so they lost. it did not matter. games come and go . . . victories and losses. but only one super bowl a year, and raymond's team had made it. our hero walking along the sidelines . . . we will never forget it.

today, taylor gets out the football and says, "i'm a patriot." he and will and brock have their huddle on the living room rug. our sons will grow up listening to us tell this story of God's miraculous blessing. we want them to understand God's unimaginable fun and adventure, if only they can hold on to His hand through times of testing and drought. we want them to know that if they never give up, sunrise always comes in time. alleluia.

♥♥
♥♥

one of the most
wonderful things about
living with children
is the memories
we store up.

already i have many memories
etched in my mind. moments
when i have stood watching taylor
and brock and have wanted that
scene never to be lost or forgotten.
other moments when i was exasperated by their behavior, yet i still
clung to the moment for the
humorous side of their childish
ingenuity.

halloween is more fun now. and
Christmas is so special with the
babies. but there are also the
simple, everyday times . . . like the
day i looked out the kitchen
window and saw taylor and brock
with their two favorite friends,
natalie, who is seven, and hilary,
nine. the girls had found three

rakes in their garages (they decided brock was too little for one). taylor, with a rake bigger than himself; brock, watching. everyone worked feverishly to create a big pile of leaves. when it was a small mountain, all four of them joined hands and jumped into the leaves with shrieks of delighted laughter. i stood perfectly still at the window and watched them do it again and again. i forgot dinner to be cooked or toys to be picked up. i tasted their warmth and love . . . feasted on my children's simplicity in enjoying life.

often now, i use hilary and natalie for baby-sitters . . . also erika. taylor and brock love them much more than they do any teenager. the girls are at the stage of playing house and living make-believe, and taking care of two babies gives them a great chance to enjoy doing that. sometimes i even have them spend the night, just for fun. they roll out their sleeping bags on the living room floor, and each one takes one of the boys to snuggle with them in front of the television.

usually i bathe the children in the evening, right before the 5 p.m. national newscast. bubble bath and toys. shampoos. i leave them in the tub for a few seconds while i move into the kitchen to check on dinner, but i keep going to peek at them without their knowing it. i listen to their noisy chatter . . . watch them soap down the tiles, sink boats, fill cups and pour bubble bath on each other's head . . . giggling all the time. always, i feel thankful to God that He gave us two, so close together. they are so much a part of each other. and they have filled our home with laughter.

one evening, after this bath-and-shampoo routine, i dressed them in clean warm pajamas. just then the phone rang, and i raced off to take a long distance

and
with
the
gift
came
laugh
·ter·

♥

call, leaving them shining-squeaky-clean, with their curls all brushed. of course i have learned to do everything with one ear alert to the boys, and as i spoke on the phone, i suddenly realized that it was very quiet . . . and had been quiet too long. too much quiet ALWAYS signals trouble.

asking the caller to wait a moment, i ran to investigate. taylor had opened the fireplace, and he and brock had crawled into the ashes that were to be cleaned out the next morning when our cleaning lady came. there were ashes everywhere! all over the hearth . . . the white carpet . . . in their hair . . . covering their faces and their clean pajamas. all i could see were two pairs of big round eyes, peering through smeared black and gray. it was the end of a long day, and the destruction looked enormous. back at the phone, i implored the caller to pray for me . . . i wondered how i could possibly salvage such a catastrophe. but of course i did . . . filling their tub with water and bubbles again, i started the entire process over. two hours later, the living room looked pretty normal, and the babies were ready for stories and bedtime.

"daddy, can we build a fire?" taylor and brock love doing this with will. they go to the basement together, and will hands each of them some pieces of kindling. i stand at the top of the stairs and watch as the big strong daddy marches up with his arms filled. behind him climbs taylor, always with two pieces in his chubby hands . . . so proud . . . trying to balance and climb without using his hands. brock trails, one little block of wood clutched in his fingers . . . equal pride on his face. i clap and cheer, and when brock gets close to the top, i always reach out and grab his

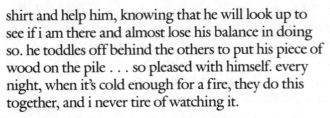

and
with
the
gift
came
laugh
·ter·

♥

shirt and help him, knowing that he will look up to see if i am there and almost lose his balance in doing so. he toddles off behind the others to put his piece of wood on the pile . . . so pleased with himself. every night, when it's cold enough for a fire, they do this together, and i never tire of watching it.

will thinks of things to do with them that are so different from my ideas, and they just love it. they are always waiting at the door, jumping and screaming, when he walks in. will bounds in with typical energy and zest, pulls off his tie and unbuttons the first couple of shirt buttons, then picks up one baby at a time. with elaborate spins and twirls, he tosses them onto the bed. finally he takes them out to the garage so they can take turns closing the garage door by pressing the two buttons on the wall.

he has taught them how to play hide and seek, hiding everywhere from the bathtub to one of the shelves in our large walk-in closet. he takes the four mahogany chairs from the little table in the bedroom and creates boats, always having an empty one for them to swim to. then they have a great storm at sea . . . he shakes their chairs with the wind, making loud noises for thunder, while they try to plow their way through pretend sleet and fog and cold to survive the storm.

using "coco" and "bobo" as star characters, he has created a series of stories for the boys. each story begins the same way: "once upon a time long, long ago in a land far, far away there lived a little boy named coco and his little brother bobo. they lived in a house painted brown and the room had white walls, just like this room. one day they asked their mother if they could go play in the backyard. she said yes. they went to the backyard and crawled into their favorite tunnel. They went down, down, down the tunnel to the land of the little people." then he tells stories of

and
with
the
gift
came
laugh
·ter·

the adventures the two little boys have with the little people. for months, i wondered why the children always wanted to play in the back and not on the large front porch. now i know they are looking for the "little people" to share their popsicles with.

jan's middle son, nash, came to spend two weeks with us. he was eight years old then, black-haired and dark-eyed, the picture of charisma and charm. every night he lived for the stories of coco and bobo, even though taylor and brock were still too small to understand it all. the saga has gone on since they were just infants and is a part of their childhood heritage.

"taylor, daddy is going to teach you how to answer the door. when someone rings the bell, or knocks, you NEVER open the door without finding out who is there. you must always ask, 'who is it?' if it is daddy, or someone else you know and trust, you can open the door. otherwise, you must never respond, but get a grownup to do it."

then they proceeded to practice it—will going outside, closing the door, and knocking. "who is it?" taylor would ask in his tiny voice. will would go through this routine, over and over, using different names. now, when we hear will's car drive in, taylor runs and locks the door so will cannot just walk in. he must knock, so that taylor can ask his question. now it is about time to teach brock the same safety rules.

of course it is exciting for me to watch my children's minds develop . . . to see their intelligent perceptions of life around them. but i am always sensitive to the mothers who have handicapped children. i see their pain as they watch all the other children magically create and progress and learn, and they compare the limited, slow progress of their own children. they long for that normal way of life for their little ones.

and
with
the
gift
came
laugh
·ter·

♥

one of the qualities i so desire for myself as a mother is to be extremely empathetic to mothers around me. it is easy to be so caught up in one's own delights that one is detached . . . blind to the needs of others. women who have never known infertility can say such careless things . . . flaunt their pregnancies . . . talk on and on about their babies in front of a woman who has never had a healthy pregnancy or been pregnant at all.

one of my most favorite things to do with taylor and brock is to bake chocolate chip cookies. i use my grandmother's wonderful recipe, and the boys sit on the counter, watching every move and eating the little bits of unbaked cookie dough i give them. every time i mention my grandmother's cookies, women ask me for the recipe, so here it is:

ANN'S GRANDMOTHER'S CHOCOLATE CHIP COOKIES

½ cup shortening (vegetable oil or melted butter)
1 cup brown sugar, packed
2 eggs
1 cup undiluted evaporated milk
1 teaspoon vanilla
2¾ cups flour
½ teaspoon baking soda
1 teaspoon salt
12-ounce package semisweet chocolate chips
1 cup chopped walnuts (optional)

mix shortening, sugar, and eggs thoroughly. add milk and vanilla. mix flour, soda, and salt together, and add to mixture. blend in chocolate chips. add nuts if desired. bake on greased cookie sheet for 10 minutes at 375 degrees.

and
with
the
gift
came
laugh
·ter·

taylor watches one program on television—mr.
rogers. for years, i would glance at his program while
changing channels and would muse about how corny
it seemed. now i am a mother, and i watch this man
in awe as he captures children by his love and caring.
he talks to them as little adults, about everything
from making record players . . . to ballet . . . to
seeing the inside of a hospital. taylor loves him and
truly believes they are actual friends. one day when
will was showing taylor a large world globe . . . point-
ing out where we live in idaho . . . and europe, where
we had all been . . . taylor suddenly looked up and
said, "daddy, show me where mr. rogers lives."

recently taylor has entered a new phase that is about
to do me in. i am not sure whether he is just totally
bored with his toys, or if it is just because he is "two-
plus." one day he came to me and said, so proudly,
"mommy, come see my room. i cleaned it!"

delighted, i followed him to his rather large room. it
did look wonderful. big and spacious . . . strangely
uncluttered, almost bare. it took me a few seconds to
realize why it looked that way. "taylor! where are all
the toys? the stuffed animals?"

proudly, he took my hand and led me toward his bed.
there is a little cubbyhole space between the head of
his crib and the wall. he had piled every puzzle piece,
every little car and truck, all the legos (in pieces), plus
twenty stuffed animals, into that space—a foot and a
half wide and four feet high. i was horror-struck, but
tried not to show it. it took me an hour, working
with him, to find every puzzle piece . . . to reorganize
the toys into their baskets—all the time scrunching
myself between the antique dresser and the wall.

and
with
the
gift
came
laugh
·ter·

the next day he piled all of this (i am not sure i am accurately conveying the picture of how much "this" is!) in the middle of the room. a huge, gigantic heap. brock, big brown eyes bigger than ever, stood there as amazed as i was. now it's easy for people to say, "make taylor clean it up," but two-year-olds can create messes that only an adult can cope with (and it helps if the adult is a genius, with a lot of spare time).

recently i was on the ragged edge. the game had gone too far, and i warned taylor that i would spank him if he did it again. later, hearing screams and laughter, i raced down the hall, fearing the worst . . . and not being one bit surprised to find it. this time taylor was in brock's crib, with brock, and all the toys were in the crib too, along with all the stuffed animals. pillows and blankets were strewn everywhere.

struggling not to lose my temper, i quietly picked up taylor and brock out of the crib. it looked to me as if it had taken both of them to create this particular mess. "all right, you two, i am going to have to spank you both. we have talked about this before."

as i started to march them to the kitchen to get the spoon, taylor began to cry. "brock didn't do it, mommy. not brock. only me!"

i turned around and looked down into his very blue eyes, filled with tears . . . his lip quivering. brock stood there, truly innocent looking. there was such courage and love and honesty in that moment. taylor loved brock too much to see him punished for something he had not done. only two years old, but he was willing to carry the blame himself. i knelt and wrapped them both in my arms. i was tired and frayed from all it takes to successfully manage two

and
with
the
gift
came
laugh
·ter·

babies, plus all my other responsibilities . . . i was a
perfectionist being chiseled down, humbled, relaxed.
i so much loved these little boys. they had not meant
to be "bad." it was just pure mischief . . . creating
fun.

"taylor, mommy is so pleased that you would not let
brock take the blame. i think i understand now that
you were just having a wonderful time. let's go back
to your room and start cleaning it up."

yes, it takes tremendous ingenuity to undo the
disaster that two toddlers can create. my mental
powers have never been so tested . . . nor my patience!

"mommy!" both taylor and brock were screaming. i
could tell they were in their bathroom . . . and i was
braced for anything—would it be a flood, dumping
water out of the toilet with cups . . . the sink with
stopper closed, full and ready to spill over? no, this
time i found taylor on the big toilet . . . all his clothes
off. he had also stripped brock of all his clothes and
had him strapped down on the little training potty.

"sit down, mommy, sit down!"

once more, i forgot the laundry to be folded, the
dishwasher to be unloaded, the breakfast mess to be
cleaned up. i even forgot that only twenty minutes
earlier, i had completely dressed them. that their dry,
unused diapers lay ruined on the bathroom floor. it
was a moment to enjoy, i decided. a moment to sit on
the little footstool and tell wonderful stories . . . and
cheer brock as, over and over, he produced a few
drops for the potty. taylor and i would congratulate
him. brock would get up, hand the potty dish to
taylor to empty, then insist on sitting down again and
trying for some more. the accolades from his audience

and
with
the
gift
came
laugh
·ter·

♥

were so enthusiastic that he was motivated to ever greater successes!

taylor's pride in brock was much more publicly shown one evening when we were preparing to go out to dinner with friends, a very dignified couple. they were waiting for us in the living room while I got the boys ready to be left with a baby-sitter. all the adults were dressed up, ready for our festive evening. quickly i changed brock's very dirty diaper on the changing counter in the kitchen. before i realized what was happening, taylor had grabbed the diaper and trotted into the living room to display brock's achievement to our guests . . . then on into the bathroom to dump the contents into the toilet. i was horrified . . . almost afraid to see what this elegant-looking couple's reaction would be, but i was reassured to see them chuckling with appreciation of taylor's good intentions.

oh, children! children are so real . . . so unveiled . . . so totally innocent . . . such clean slates. it is awesome and sobering, wanting to write into their lives all the pure and strong and healthy feelings and philosophies. yet we are older . . . tarnished by impurity, bigotry, half-truths, the compromises of the world.

every day as we put the babies into the car, taylor always begs brock to let him hold his hand. brock is very independent. besides, he usually has been pushed around by taylor ten minutes before, so he may not be in the mood for holding hands! will and i have tried to lessen taylor's determination to do this, for we do not believe brock should be forced to hold his hand. recently the scene took place again. i strapped each boy into his car seat, then i crawled in and fastened my seat belt, ready to turn on the car. as

and
with
the
gift
came
laugh
·ter·

♥

usual, taylor was in tears because brock did not want to hold his hand. i was stern . . . then gentle . . . then i begged brock to give in.

"brock, hold taylor's hand, honey. he is your brother. he loves you." they were both wearing their dressy coats and smart little john-john hats, with curls framing their faces. finally even brock erupted into tears from the pressure. i decided i would be quiet and let them work it out themselves, so i drove on.

the light turned red. stopping, i turned around to look at those cherubic faces. suddenly brock reached out his little hand to take taylor's.

"hi," he smiled, tears still on his cheeks.

"hi," taylor responded, also with tear-streaked face.

another moment . . . etched in my mind, never to be forgotten. tenderness and love poured out, filling the empty places. two happy babies, clinging to each other's hand all the way to our destination. there is nothing like children to unite hard, cold hearts and wipe out prejudices. save your memories . . . store them in your heart for all time to come.

"Father God, take will and me. keep us pure enough and wise enough to know how to guide our little sons. make us honest, so that—in spite of their flaws—they will be brave and strong . . . with free, unfettered spirits to affect the world. fill us with Your presence . . . Your truth."

♥♥
♥♥

one morning will called home from his office.

"ann, i have to go to washington, d.c., on business. it's important that i be there today. how about you and the boys picking me up at noon, and we can visit enroute to the airport."

"okay, honey. how long will you be gone?" i asked.

"only two or three days. i will be home for the weekend."

i dressed the babies in their handsome hats and coats, buckled them in, and drove downtown. will was buoyant and enthusiastic when he got into the car. he chatted with taylor and brock . . . talked to me about this particular business deal. when i pulled up to the curb at the airport, will leaned over and kissed me, then got out of the car and opened each back door and

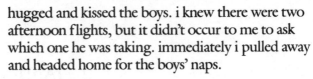

hugged and kissed the boys. i knew there were two afternoon flights, but it didn't occur to me to ask which one he was taking. immediately i pulled away and headed home for the boys' naps.

as always, i put a sign on the front door that said, "babies are sleeping; please come back later." i also took the phone off the hook and climbed into bed to read and take a nap while the babies were asleep.

two hours later i replaced the receiver on the phone, and instantly it rang. "ann! oh, ann, i am so glad you answered the phone," announced my friend melissa. "i was so afraid you might have been on that plane that crashed between here and salt lake city this afternoon."

numb, frozen with fear, i choked out, "what plane?"

"haven't you heard the news?" melissa said, now sounding very relieved and relaxed. "it was that skywest flight."

my head was spinning. i could not believe that i had so casually dropped will off at the airport, not even asking about the specifics of his flight. had i heard him say something about skywest?

"melissa, i am safe, but will did take an afternoon flight east. please . . . can i call you back?" i spoke quietly, as calmly as possible.

standing alone in my kitchen . . . taylor and brock still sleeping . . . i was almost incapable of movement. i wanted to know the truth, yet i was horrified at what it might be. how could i raise these two little boys by myself? they would be cheated out of so much if something happened to will. they adored him so, and he just played a totally different role in their lives than

and
with
the
gift
came
laugh
·ter·

i did. one thing for sure . . . i would never marry again if will were gone. there just aren't any other men on the face of the earth like him. he is unique . . . and i had waited thirty-five years to find him.

with trembling fingers i dialed our travel agency. lynette, the one we especially like to do business with there, answered. she is so special to us, and we trust her implicitly.

"lynette. . . ." i could hardly speak.

"ann," she said in a hushed tone. her voice made me wonder if she was saying how sorry she was that will was gone.

"lynette, was will on that skywest?" i asked through dry throat and lips.

"ann, didn't you know that when we discovered skywest was having some problems and would be delayed, we immediately switched will over to the western flight? i just supposed you knew. we are all really shaken up here, though."

i fell on my knees by the kitchen counter, tears streaming down my face. my heart was filled with praise and honor and thanksgiving—and overwhelming relief. i called melissa to let her know will was okay, and shortly thereafter, the babies awakened from their naps. my phone rang constantly the rest of the day. the city newspaper had heard, "from undisclosed sources," that will's life had been spared. could they do an interview with me? the television stations began calling. they wanted me on the evening and late news.

the situation turned from a near tragedy to a great opportunity for me to say some things, and the

and
with
the
gift
came
laugh
·ter·

♥

world was eager to listen. repeatedly i told of will's
going to meet with a representative of a foreign
country in the nation's capital . . . the shock and
despair i felt when news of the crash came to
me . . . the tremendous relief when i knew will was
okay . . . the fervent, deep faith that will and i have
about the providences of God.

"will has called me," i told one television reporter,
"and we have talked a lot about God's sovereignty
and care over us. we realize nothing can harm us until
God is through with us, and there are very few things
in life that *really* matter—certainly not a big business
deal. it's having each other and our two little boys. the
love we share . . . the simple memories of fun together, playing with our children, and the feel of
small, trusting hands clinging to ours."

at that point, the television cameras began to scan the
little pairs of shoes lined up on the kitchen counter
and the toys in the corner of the room. "we believe,"
i continued, "that God still has more for will to do,
and we are humbled and grateful beyond words."

this was not the first time will had missed a plane
crash. ten or eleven years earlier, his family was in los
angeles for the graduation of his sister chrisie from
the art school where she received her graduate degree.
will and his father were to return sunday afternoon
on an airwest flight. the traffic was bad, so will's
father said, "let's relax and go back tomorrow morning."

after a good night's sleep, will and his dad read the
shocking morning headlines. the very flight they
were to have taken had collided with a navy plane.
both planes had crashed and there were no survivors
on their flight.

and
with
the
gift
came
laugh
·ter·

♥

life is a vapor. it is fleeting. one of the most significant
things we feel we can instill in our children—next to
a solid, deep faith in God—is the ability to be happy
in the present. happiness is something most people
have to learn, for we tend to look to the past, or live
for the future.

when i was a child, i used to sing the little chorus,
"everybody happy, say AMEN!" it mattered so much
to me that my family be happy, right where we were,
and if one member was not very enthusiastic, i would
pursue it until he or she said, "amen!" now my
toddlers sing the same song and laugh as they shout,
"AMEN!"

right where you are today, be happy. we impede the
creative flow of God when we are always anxious and
wanting something better . . . a bigger house . . .
more financial security . . . a child . . . a better job
. . . where we used to live instead of where we are. as
i learned to enjoy being with will in idaho falls, and
to accept my miscarriages and losses, i began to feel
healing. it was when i became content, right where
i was, that God brought me will anderson . . . and
taylor . . . and brock.

we are trying to teach our little boys the joy of simple
fun. not to overindulge them so that their happiness
and security become dependent upon possessions and
privileges. on taylor's first Christmas, we bought him
only one gift . . . a $5.99 stepladder from the hard-
ware store. we knew he would be getting gifts from
grandparents and friends, and we do not believe in
too much of anything *except* love and acceptance and
forgiveness. amazingly, the stepladder has been his
favorite thing for two years.

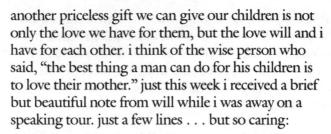

and
with
the
gift
came
laugh
·ter·

another priceless gift we can give our children is not only the love we have for them, but the love will and i have for each other. i think of the wise person who said, "the best thing a man can do for his children is to love their mother." just this week i received a brief but beautiful note from will while i was away on a speaking tour. just a few lines . . . but so caring:

dear ann . . . you are somewhere back east and i am
    at the office. thinking of how i love you. . . .
i love your blue eyes.
i love your affirming spirit.
i love your attention to details.
i love your good food.
i love your handling of the boys.
i love your heart.
i love everything about you!! will

one day i was holding a month-old baby while the young mother was eating at a luncheon in her honor. taylor and brock went wild over this baby, kissing him . . . putting a finger in his tiny hand for him to squeeze . . . patting the baby's back. they were beside themselves with delight over this little baby.

"taylor, would you like another baby at our house?" i asked.

"yes . . . and God will do it!" he announced, with a two-year-old's dignity and confidence.

"and God will do it!" how profound. children must learn to believe that God is good. that God is our Hope, our Refuge. theirs, too. life is filled with injustices, but a child can be happy and strong if he believes that with time, God can make the difference.

we would love to have one or two more children. there are probably things you desire, too. if your desire is really what is best for you, God will do it. for today, though, just be happy with all the good He already has done. let contentment cover your home and fill your heart . . . and the world will be changed.

Our children too shall serve him,
for they shall hear from us
about the wonders of the Lord;
generations yet unborn shall hear
of all the miracles he did for us.
Psalm 22:30-31 THE LIVING BIBLE